AF715453

Cloud-Based Services for Your Library

ALA TechSource purchases fund advocacy, awareness, and accreditation programs for library professionals worldwide.

lita

Cloud-Based Services for Your Library

A LITA Guide

Erik T. Mitchell

ALA TechSource
An imprint of the American Library Association

CHICAGO 2013

ERIK MITCHELL is an assistant professor at the College of Information Studies at the University of Maryland, College Park. In addition to studying information technology adoption and use in libraries, Erik examines metadata issues and professional development in library and information science. Before joining the University of Maryland, Erik served as the assistant director for Technology Services in the Z. Smith Reynolds Library at Wake Forest University, where he worked for twelve years. During this time he coordinated the development, implementation, and management of a variety of library systems and most recently was responsible for the migration of the Reynolds Library IT services to cloud-based platforms. Erik is a columnist for the *Journal of Web Librarianship* and has published and presented on library IT, metadata use, and pedagogical approaches. He holds a PhD in information and library science from the University of North Carolina at Chapel Hill, an MLS from the University of South Carolina, and a BA in literature from Lenoir-Rhyne College.

© 2013 by the American Library Association. Any claim of copyright is subject to applicable limitations and exceptions, such as rights of fair use and library copying pursuant to Sections 107 and 108 of the U.S. Copyright Act. No copyright is claimed for content in the public domain, such as works of the U.S. government.

Printed in the United States of America

17 16 15 14 13 5 4 3 2 1

Extensive effort has gone into ensuring the reliability of the information in this book; however, the publisher makes no warranty, express or implied, with respect to the material contained herein.

ISBNs: 978-1-55570-878-8 (paper); 978-1-55570-900-6 (PDF); 978-1-55570-901-3 (ePub); 978-1-55570-902-0 (Kindle). For more information on digital formats, visit the ALA Store at alastore.ala.org and select eEditions.

Library of Congress Cataloging-in-Publication Data

Mitchell, Erik T., 1972-
Cloud-Based Services for Your Library / Erik T. Mitchell.
pages cm. — (A LITA guide)
Includes bibliographical references and index.
ISBN 978-1-55570-878-8
1. Web services—Library applications. 2. Cloud computing. 3. Electronic information resources—Management. 4. Internet programming. I. Library and Information Technology Association (U.S.) II. Title.
Z674.75.W67M58 2013
025.04—dc23 2012040838

Book design in Berkeley and Avenir. Cover image ©Lightspring/Shutterstock, Inc.

♾ This paper meets the requirements of ANSI/NISO Z39.48-1992 (Permanence of Paper).

For Mom, Dad,
Lisa and Jeff.
Thank you.

Contents

Preface

In 2009, I began the process of migrating the IT infrastructure of Wake Forest University's Z. Smith Reynolds Library to "the cloud." We moved to the cloud because we believed our library IT systems needed to be as flexible as the services we wanted to deliver, and we suspected that the cloud, although not necessarily cheaper at that point in time, would help us be more agile in the coming years. We were also committed to open-source solutions and viewed the cloud as an environment that would enable us to work with the best open-source library information systems. I took on this migration with the support of my colleagues at the library, a collaborative spirit with campus IT, a good measure of vendor support for our proprietary systems, and healthy doses of optimism and openness toward what the cloud is and what it would take to be successful. Over the course of a year my technology team and I learned much about cloud architecture, system administration, application administration, and IT service for libraries.

My goal in writing this book is to help libraries considering cloud computing to start their exploration of these systems with a more informed perspective. In speaking with librarians I found that, although many libraries shared our enthusiasm, there was little in the way of formal works and guidance available to help them on this path. Because of this need, this book explores the broad area of virtualization and cloud computing adoption but makes an effort to focus on their use in library environments. To do this, I take a wide-reaching approach by defining cloud computing, by examining models to assess its adoption in libraries, and by exploring specific examples of cloud computing and virtualization to serve as a practical guide.

AUDIENCE AND SCOPE

This book is written for both librarians and IT staff. It includes broad discussions about legal and policy issues as well as specific information about the technical requirements, capabilities, and limitations of different cloud approaches. In chapters 4 and 5 there are sections that define basic technical concepts as well as discussion sections that examine the range of skills and IT service capacity required to implement each solution. One of the goals of this book is to help bridge the gap between technical and organizational issues in technology adoption and to suggest approaches that work well in a virtualized environment.

This book provides readers with several cloud computing frameworks, potential real-world solutions, and evaluative models to assess the fit of these items with their own organization, concluding with an exploration of potential virtualization and cloud computing approaches for libraries and a discussion of examples already in use in the library world. In getting the reader to this point, the book seeks to answer some of the central questions in technology evaluation. For example, chapter 2 examines the state of cloud computing adoption in academic libraries, and chapter 3 builds on this work to explore the process of evaluating the impact of technical, organizational, and environmental factors when selecting an IT platform. Using the factors identified in chapter 2, the exploration of cloud computing approaches in chapters 3 and 4 examine issues specific to each platform (e.g., SaaS, PaaS and IaaS), staff expertise requirements, methods for evaluating service cost, and factors important in evaluating the service including complexity, reliability, sustainability, portability, and interoperability. In addition to discussing these concepts in relation to specific approaches, chapter 3 addresses factors important in cloud and virtualization adoption using the "technology, organization and environment" (TOE) model explored in chapter 2, including IT service management issues and IT service adoption issues such as expertise, budgeting and expense analysis, legal/policy factors, and service level agreements. Though not a complete replacement for a full work on IT service management or the legal and organizational issues relevant to a move to a new IT environment, the chapter provides readers with a framework with which to examine issues critical to the success of the cloud in their environment.

The material in this book was drawn from numerous sources, including my expertise in cloud adoption, a survey of library-specific uses of cloud computing, relevant literature in IT service management, vendor interviews, platform testing, and technical and case study literature in the library IT field. Although I selected particular projects, vendors, and platforms to highlight, I also found that the number of systems and options in this area is growing rapidly, so it is likely that some popular systems and services are not covered in this book.

ORGANIZATION OF MATERIAL

Chapter 1 defines virtualization and cloud computing, examines specific solutions for these platforms, and discusses some common approaches to platform adoption. This chapter examines cloud computing models and uses these models to set up the discussion in the remainder of the book.

Chapter 2 reports the results of a survey of virtualization and cloud computing adoption in libraries. The survey was conducted in the fall of 2011, and the data were analyzed using technology adoption models. The findings of this chapter are an empirical grounding for the model used to examine specific cloud computing solutions in the remainder of the book.

Chapter 3 explores factors and issues related to IT adoption in detail. The chapter is grouped by technical, organizational, and environmental factors and takes the reader through system evaluation and implementation planning. This chapter also includes a focus on the role of IT service management in system design.

Chapter 4 examines software-as-a-service (SaaS) and platform-as-a-service (PaaS) solutions that are relevant to library information systems. The chapter includes an overview of relevant technical concepts, an exploration of information systems that use SaaS, and an examination of factors that influence decision making for these services.

Like chapter 4, chapter 5 examines cloud services but focuses specifically on infrastructure-as-a-service (IaaS) and multiplatform solutions. The chapter includes an overview of relevant technical concepts, an exploration of information systems that use IaaS, and an examination of factors that influence decision making for these services.

Chapter 6 reviews the models explored in the book and the systems examined in chapters 4 and 5 and presents four generic models that can be used in system design: an entire SaaS environment, a pure IaaS environment, and two models that explore the creation of a mixed-model approach. The chapter concludes with suggestions for incorporating cloud computing and virtualization into your IT environment.

Acknowledgments

The motivation to write this book began with the idea that libraries are best served when their adoption of IT matches the speed and flexibility of their service needs. In exploring how to accomplish this using cloud computing, I relied on the knowledge of my fellow librarians, the know-how and patience of IT experts, and the support of my colleagues at the Z. Smith Reynolds Library at Wake Forest University. Special thanks go to Tim Mitchell, Kevin Gilbertson, and Barry Davis, who all took the leap into cloud computing with me and who made the cloud a success at our library. Thank you as well to Susan Smith, Lynn Sutton, and the entire staff and faculty of the library, whose trust of our team made it all possible. Thanks go to my helpful colleagues from across the Wake Forest campus, including Paul Whitener, Jeremy Kindy, Seth Stein, and Odi Lancu, whose knowledge, patience, and collaboration made our experiment with cloud computing a reality.

In researching for and writing this book I relied on the expertise and feedback of my conference workshop participants and the members of online library communities, including Code4Lib and LITA. Thank you for your new ideas and technical advice. Thank you also to the participants of the adoption survey, who provided me with a wider understanding of cloud adoption in libraries. I also had the chance to talk with communities from around the country about my work and am grateful to them for listening and for the generosity of their feedback. Many thanks go to my editor, Marta Deyrup, whose patience and guidance kept this book moving through a world of change and to the Neal-Schuman team who got this book to press. Thanks also go to my colleagues at the College of Information Studies at the University of Maryland, who helped me keep writing as I started a new chapter of my career. Finally, I could not have written this book without the inspiration and support of Jeffery Loo, whose mentorship, capacity for help, and uncanny ability to create an insightful conclusion from a jumble of ideas made this book what it is.

Chapter One

Cloud Computing and Virtualization in Libraries

The adoption of cloud computing in libraries is part of a larger trend of library innovation that is changing how libraries allocate financial, IT, and personnel resources. This shift both is driven by and is influencing other areas of library operations, including cataloging and metadata management, digital information services, community contribution to information spaces, and digital collections management. Like all of these trends, cloud computing and virtualization can fundamentally transform not only how libraries provide services but also how they define their core and value-added functions. Just as the delivery of the Internet as a public service in libraries transformed patron views of libraries, new trends of networked bibliographic data, an increasing demand for digital reference services, and the emergence of electronic collections are again changing both the services and their delivery method. These changes are motivating libraries to find ways to make information technology more efficient, more diffused throughout library operations, and more flexible in a changing environment. Cloud computing and its parent—virtualization—are helping libraries shape their services and collections toward these goals and, as this book shows, pose unique challenges and opportunities for libraries.

The opportunities that come from these technologies are unique for libraries because libraries are themselves unique from other information institutions. Libraries balance the roles of public service and cultural preservation. They often operate under the auspices of parent organizations and often find themselves functioning within the context of local technical, budgetary, and operational constraints. Libraries frequently license or purchase services with the sole intent of giving them away in the most efficient and customer-friendly way possible. Just as there is no one type of library, there is no single reason why libraries turn to virtual or cloud-based services. Perhaps the most common motivation comes from resource constraints or an interest in new and innovative service. Other times it comes from a desire to deliver high-quality information services that surpass the capacity of local IT infrastructure or expertise. In these approaches libraries are embracing the spirit of start-up organizations, adapting to changing business models, taking a "permanent-beta" approach to service deployment, focusing on underserved populations and opportunities, and shifting resources toward successful experiments.

Over the past twenty years library services have become increasingly tied to Internet-based technologies. Though beneficial to library patrons, the delivery of Internet and other computing resources along with traditional library services is increasingly difficult to sustain (Bertot et al. 2011). In efforts to build on IT-rich services and reach diverse populations in new ways, libraries are experimenting with social media and mobile applications (Blowers 2010), seeking new IT platforms for services (Schrier 2011), migrating traditional systems to cloud-based environments (Breeding 2011b; Fitzpatrick 2010), using cloud-based services to engage student populations (Behrend et al. 2011), and investigating new approaches to digital libraries that include network-scale information systems (Kimpton and Baker 2011).

OVERVIEW OF CLOUD COMPUTING AND VIRTUALIZATION

Cloud computing and virtualization are complementary technologies which, although technically very different, are often seen as similar approaches to solving a common problem. This book examines both concepts because a decision to either virtualize an IT service or deploy it in a cloud environment comes down to issues of service scale, organizational factors, or institutional capacity rather than to issues of the technologies themselves. For example, although many libraries choose to outsource link resolution services, libraries that have complex internal data needs that do not fit the data models of hosted OpenURL service providers often run this service in-house. This example points to a real-world issue that is important to note early in this book—that libraries often discuss outsourced and hosted services using the terminology of cloud computing and virtualization. Although the technical definitions of virtualization and cloud computing are very different from the operational definitions of outsourcing and service hosting, this book intentionally blurs the lines between cloud-based approaches such as software as a service (SaaS) and SaaS-style service hosting as provided by library IT vendors. This allows us to compare these approaches and to discuss the creation of an IT service infrastructure that more closely matches the diverse suite of providers and platforms that is typical in libraries. Discussing outsourcing and hosting in terms of their cloud-based and virtualized IT counterparts also provides us with opportunities to assess the technical and service quality of hosted and outsourced services using common IT measures. To begin our exploration of these broad topics, we must define and consider the differences between cloud computing and virtualization.

CLOUD COMPUTING

Two organizations, Gartner and the National Institute of Standards and Technology (NIST), are regarded as having created well-formed definitions of cloud computing. Both approach this definition by discussing different facets of cloud computing services (Mell and Grance 2011; Smith 2010). NIST broadly defines cloud computing as "a model for enabling ubiquitous, convenient, on-demand network access to a shared pool of configurable computing resources (e.g., networks, servers, storage, applications and services) that can be rapidly provisioned and released with minimal management effort or service provider interaction" (Hogan et al. 2011). It additionally qualifies cloud computing through the use of three service models: SaaS, platform as a service (PaaS), and infrastructure as a service (IaaS). The NIST cloud computing framework defines features common to all cloud computing environments and differentiates cloud service models from cloud deployment models (Mell and Grance 2011).

Table 1.1 lists the characteristics and models of the NIST definition of a cloud environment. It is useful to understand that, although cloud solutions all employ a service model, a deployment model, and service features, each solution will likely include a different combination of service features and deployment models. For example, both Microsoft Azure and Amazon Web Services (AWS) offer a mix of PaaS and IaaS solutions, and RightScale and Rackspace help users bridge between public and private clouds. In addition, it is increasingly common for cloud

TABLE 1.1
NIST Elements of Cloud Computing

Essential characteristic	Service model	Deployment model
On demand self-service	SaaS	Private cloud
Broad network access	PaaS	Community cloud
Resource pooling	IaaS	Public cloud
Rapid elasticity		Hybrid cloud
Measured or metered		

providers to define custom cloud solutions for security, IT management, identity management, and other information services using the "as-a-service" model. This fragmentation can make it difficult for users to differentiate service types and points to the complex set of relationships that underlie a given cloud service.

Essential Characteristics

The NIST model features several essential characteristics that can be used to help differentiate cloud services. These characteristics describe an environment in which IT services can be allocated by the end user (e.g., on-demand self service), can be scaled as needed (e.g., rapid elasticity), and which are paid for by a subscription as opposed to a one-time purchase fee (e.g., measured service). NIST essential characteristics also describe an environment in which services are available across the network and IT resources are colocated to facilitate sharing and scaling. In contrast, traditional IT environments focus on locally hosted hardware purchased through one-time capital expenditures, planned as opposed to on-demand capacity, and static or more slowly changed service offerings. It is important to consider these features (e.g., elasticity, scalability, on-demand) when examining cloud solutions, but it is equally important to consider which features are preferable for a given service. For example, in the library marketplace outsourced or hosted IT services and dedicated SaaS providers often offer cloud services that are neither on-demand nor elastic but which may make use of these characteristics to create and manage their underlying cloud infrastructure.

Service Models

SaaS, PaaS, and IaaS service models are the most common ones discussed in cloud computing definitions, but there are situations in which the distinctions between them are unclear. The "as-a-service" approach to cloud computing includes database as a service (DaaS; Howe et al. 2011), security as a service (SECaas; Hussain and Abdulsalam 2011), and identity as a service (Krüger and Grabski 2009). The reuse of acronyms as well as a broadening of definitions in cloud computing can make it difficult for information organizations to identify and select services. At the same time, companies are able to provide niche services that would be difficult or too expensive for smaller organizations to implement. For example, CloudFlare (www.cloudflare.com) protects against denial of service and traffic load spikes by managing domain name service (DNS) and service replication across multiple cloud providers without the required load balancing and security configuration required for this type of service. By taking advantage of such a service, an information organization can built robustness into its IT configuration without the costs that would have been a necessity in more traditional IT environments. As our exploration of these service models in chapters 4 and 5 shows, the model a library chooses largely depends on factors such as local expertise, IT service requirements, organizational policy, and local preference.

Deployment Models

NIST's four deployment models (Fang et al. 2011) differentiate internal and external environments and examine approaches to cloud computing that serve specific communities. In this model, private clouds are defined as an environment in which the customer has exclusive physical or virtual access to its computing services. These services may be on-site or remotely hosted by a cloud provider, but typically they involve dedicated hardware and are available only via private physical or virtual networks. In community cloud environments a group of related customers have shared access to computing services. Although the actual computing services may be run in-house or by the cloud provider, community clouds tend to feature shared access to some or all resources in the cloud environment. Government clouds or educational clouds are good examples of community and private clouds. These environments may be run on dedicated hardware and networks, as in the case of private clouds, but may also be run on hardware that serves other cloud customers but with virtual isolation. The Amazon government computing cloud is just one of many community/private cloud solutions available. In contrast to private and community clouds, public cloud solutions feature a cloud-computing service and infrastructure that is made available to the general public. Though public cloud platforms are open to all subscribers, they often feature security layers that allow subscribers to create virtually private environments that are as secure as private clouds. For example, the AWS platform operates largely as a public cloud solution but is designed so that customer IT resources are virtually isolated from Amazon employees and other subscribers. Hybrid clouds are the "catch-all" of models in that they include features of two or more types of cloud systems (public, private, or community) but are bound together for data or application sharing.

There are both risks and advantages of scale that go with each deployment approach. For instance, in environments where physical security and virtual privacy are of utmost importance, public clouds are likely not the best solution. Likewise, where economies of scale and interoperability are important, private clouds are not likely to be best suited. It is important to be familiar with these models; understanding them helps contextualize options for cloud computing adoption. Good explanations that focus on the intersection between service models and deployment models have been prepared by various authors (Mell and Grance 2011; Metz 2011) and further inform on the differences between them.

In addition to understanding the distinction between service and deployment models, it is important to understand the roles of cloud providers and subscribers. These include common roles such as cloud adopter and cloud provider as well as emerging roles such as cloud auditor and cloud broker. The NIST reference model in figure 1.1 shows the relationships among these participants and explores the

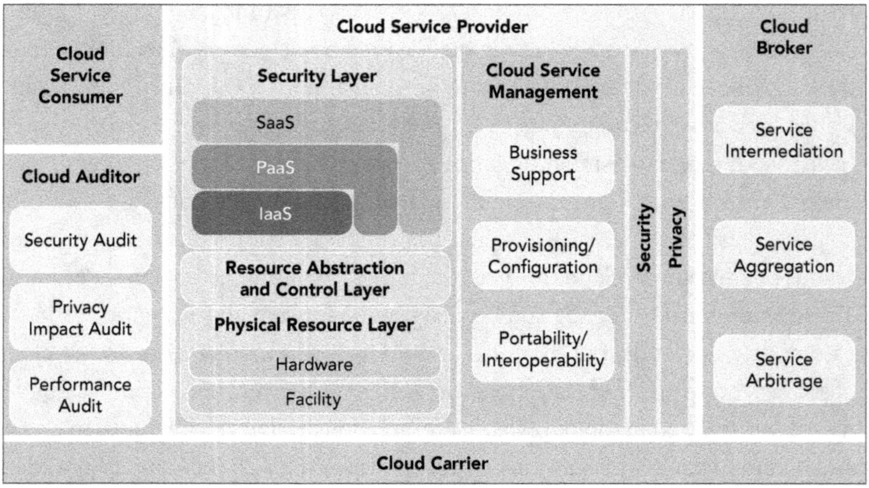

FIGURE 1.1
NIST cloud reference model

relationship between activities (e.g., cloud use, development, deployment) and auditing, managing, and functions such as service deployment, resource allocation, and physical/virtual security.

The NIST model also defines the limits of expertise and responsibility that should be expected of the various players in a cloud computing solution. It is worth noting that the roles of consumer, auditor, provider, carrier, and broker may not apply in all cloud computing adoption frameworks; nevertheless, they are valuable roles to consider when exploring new IT systems. For example, in many cases libraries (e.g., the cloud consumer) interact directly with cloud providers rather than working through a cloud broker. In this case the process of working with and auditing service layers, security, privacy, and service-level agreements (SLAs) falls on the cloud consumer. The NIST model also provides a taxonomy of cloud features (Fang et al. 2011) that describes the issues cloud consumers should be aware of when selecting and implementing a cloud solution. This taxonomy defines the activities (e.g., service creation, publishing, auditing), components (e.g., processes, actions, tasks), and subcomponents (e.g., service provision, service decommission) that may be helpful for organizations seeking to understand relationships and interactions important in cloud computing adoption.

VIRTUALIZATION

In contrast to cloud computing, virtualization is defined as "the abstraction of IT resources in a way that masks the physical nature and boundaries of those resources from resource users" (Gartner 2011). Virtualization enables creation of multiple virtual machines on a shared hardware platform; enhances flexibility in CPU, memory, and storage allocations between machines; and is designed to be portable across hardware platforms (Smith and Nair 2005). This is a broad definition that includes the virtualization of servers, clients, network-attached storage, and any number of other computing resources. Common server platforms include XEN (http://xen.org), Citrix (http://citrix.com), and VMware (http://vmware.com). Each virtualization platform has historically supported its own virtualization format (e.g., Kernel Virtual Machine, Bare Metal, VMWare VMDK), but there is also a movement to support an open virtualization standard that would enable easy interoperability among virtualization platforms. These solutions can be a valuable tool for libraries, but they often come with a requirement for technical infrastructure and expertise that commonly is not held by libraries.

In this section I differentiate client- and server-based virtualization, but there are client virtualization platforms (e.g.,VirtualBox) that are also used in a server environment to provide remote access to multiple virtualized clients. This use meets a wide range of needs including creating specialized instruction environments (Thomas and Whitener 2010), deploying virtualized desktop computing environments (Baev et al. 2011), and facilitating the support for legacy applications (Wong 2008). Another common use of virtualization is to provide virtual computing labs (VCL; Shaffer et al. 2009). This approach often uses the Apache Software Foundation's VCL platform (https://cwiki.apache.org/VCL/) to provide a robust virtualized lab environment that is capable of serving both dedicated physical and virtual machines.

Virtualization systems are managed by an application called a hypervisor that manages multiple virtual machines in a single server or across multiple physical servers. There are both commercial and open-source hypervisor platforms and multiple approaches to hardware and virtual server management within these platforms. Some hypervisors such as Xen (http://xen.org) include the ability to add and remove computing resources easily without affecting specific virtual machine deployments. This form of virtualization is more accurately referred to as private cloud computing and is often deployed in an IT configuration that is physically very different from single-server virtualized platforms. Systems that focus on private cloud environments include advanced resource and service management features and may support "bursting" from a private cloud to a public cloud deployment.

Marko's (2012, 8) taxonomy of cloud systems includes abstracted management services for five types of subsystems including computing resources, storage resources, server imaging, identity management, and a management dashboard. Some common platforms that include these features are OpenStack (http://openstack.org), CloudStack (http://cloudstack.org), and Eucalyptus (http://eucalyptus.com). These products also often employ application programming interface (API) toolkits that enable efficient and automated management and may integrate with a public cloud provider. By featuring a common API language, private cloud platforms make it easy to deploy services on both private and public cloud platforms and can even enable automated bridging of services from a private cloud to a public cloud. For example, OpenStack is the platform supporting RackSpace, and many products support a common set of operations such as "create machine," "start/stop machine," and "terminate machine." One provider in particular (Eucalyptus) has formal agreements with Amazon to ensure interoperability between system APIs, and so software written to interact with one service is portable to the other.

Virtualization is often thought of in terms of server environments, but it is also increasingly used in client environments. In client computing, virtualization is typically used to provide access to multiple operating systems (e.g., a Linux virtual machine run inside a Windows environment) or to enable use of a specific tool or application. Some benefits of client virtualization include easy testing of multiple operating systems, use of clients with different platform requirements, and compartmentalization of complex computing environments. Popular client virtualization platforms include VirtualBox (http://virtualbox.org), Parallels (http://parallels.com), Microsoft Virtual PC (www.microsoft.com/windows/virtual-pc), and VMware Fusion (http://vmware.com).

Virtualization technology has become more popular in recent years and more adept at providing seamless native application functionality in a multiple operating system environment. For example, both Parallels and VirtualBox offer the capability to run applications as if they were native applications on the host operating system (Purdy 2010). Figure 1.2 shows two virtual client machines (Windows and Ubuntu) running inside a VirtualBox hypervisor. Client hypervisors support both direct use on the hardware platform and remote usage via Remote Desktop Protocol

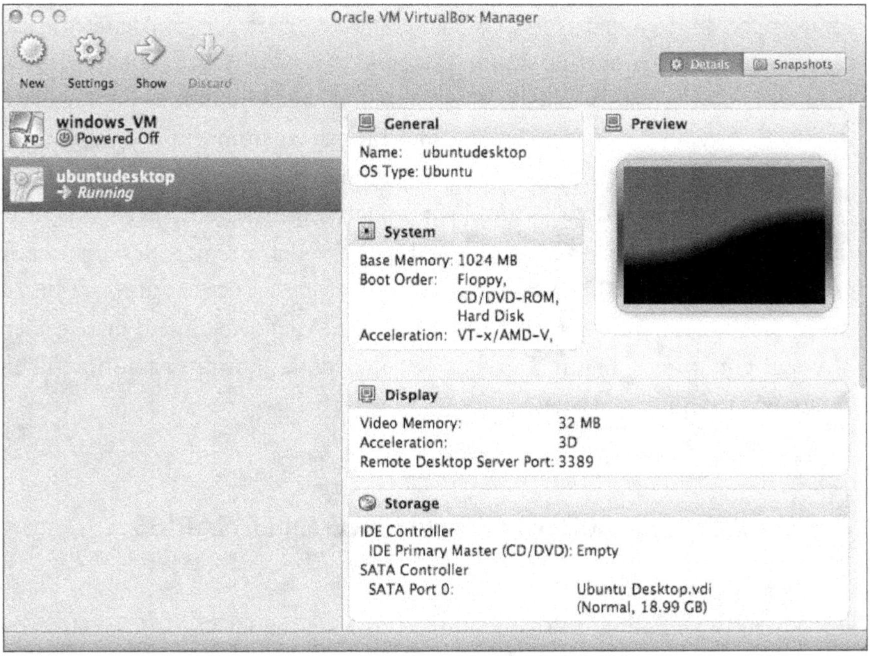

FIGURE 1.2
VirtualBox hypervisor

or Virtual Network Connection. Client-based virtual computing is used to provide preconfigured test environments for open-source library information systems. For example, Islandora, a customized platform running on top of Drupal, Solr, GSearch, and the Fedora digital library system provides a downloadable virtual machine (http://islandora.ca/download). The image published by Islandora uses the Open Virtualization format (OVA) that makes it possible to deploy the virtualized image in any virtualization platform that supports this standard. Likewise, the open-source ILS Evergreen is available in developer and production OVA images (www.open-ils.org/downloads.php#evergreen_vm), and Archivematica (http://archivematica.org) provides both Live DVD (a bootable DVD) and OVA images. By providing test environments on common virtualization platforms, these platforms make it possible for libraries to explore systems without large amounts of technical experience or infrastructure.

Generally speaking, virtualization is seen as a means to reduce IT expenditures, improve access to computing environments, and provide advanced computing services to end users (Miller 2009). New adopters of virtualization may feel that they are a long way from realizing these benefits. Because VirtualBox supports a variety of client- and server-specific tools, it can be a good starting point for libraries seeking to provide a local or small-scale virtualized service. This can facilitate testing open-source library services (e.g., Islandora, Evergreen, or Archivematica), experimenting with new operating systems, and becoming familiar with the hardware and software elements of virtualization. In addition to a graphical user interface, VirtualBox also supports a command line environment and a "headless" virtual machine mode. In headless mode, the virtual machine does not launch in an application window on the host machine but rather is accessible only through network protocols (e.g., accessed only through a remote desktop or SSH connection) (Oracle 2012). Headless mode clients use fewer computing resources on the host server and offer ways to automate the deployment and management of client computers. Figure 1.3 shows the terminal output of multiple-client computers running in headless mode.

IT SERVICE AND CLOUD COMPUTING IN LIBRARIES

The rapid pace of change in libraries is affecting IT service needs in both the library and parent organization. It is common for decisions about IT platform adoption and administration to be the purview of IT departments that primarily serve

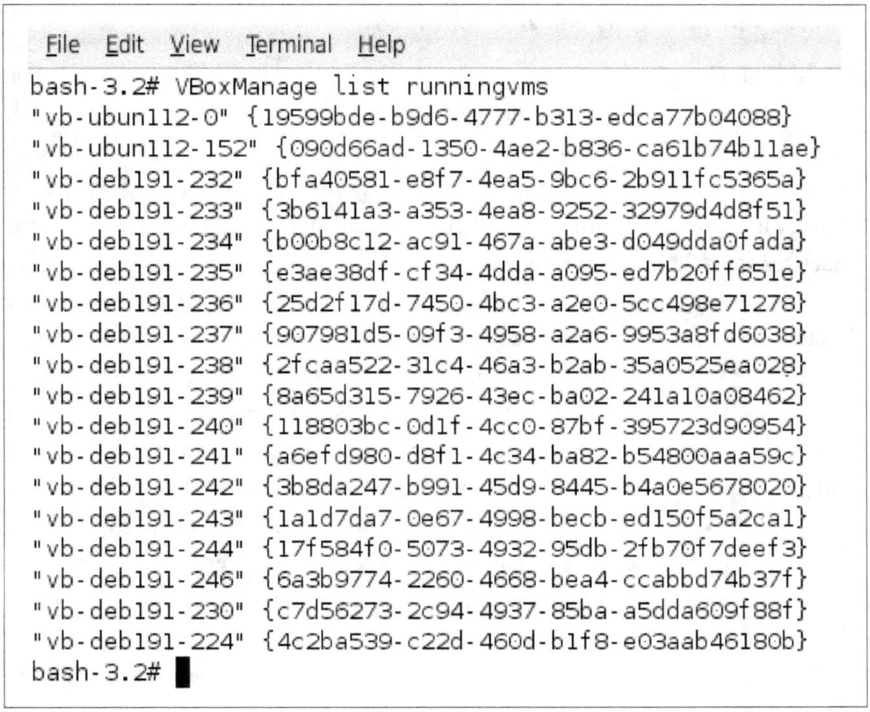

FIGURE 1.3
VirtualBox in headless mode

the parent organization rather than the library. This can mean that important IT decisions are made at an organizational rather than departmental level, including selection of server hardware, operating systems, and software stacks—all of which influence software selection in other areas of the organization. This situation has the potential to limit the IT solutions libraries can pursue when exploring new systems and can be frustrating as libraries adopt new digital services.

At the same time, libraries are adopting systems that include large-scale data management components and are turning to a wider range of information service providers. Systems such as electronic resource management systems and recommender services are key examples of data-rich services being implemented in new Data as a Service (DAAS) solutions. For Breeding, this trend toward expanded services and new ILSs "addresses the fundamental changes that libraries have experienced over the course of the last decade or so toward more engagement with electronic and digital content" (2011a).

Factors Influencing Service Choices

The shift in IT implementation practices away from traditional in-house solutions to cloud-based, hosted, or outsourced solutions means that libraries must consider new issues when making IT selections. Fortunately, libraries have practice in working with contract negotiation, online service evaluation, data access and preservation, subscription pricing models, and network-based authentication practices from their experience in migrating to digital subscription-based research tools and e-journals (Zambare et al. 2009). This is particularly true in the case of library electronic content licenses, which often include assurances on technical elements of the service. Key aspects of the standard license terms for resources licensed by the California Digital Library, for example, include server availability and performance criteria, authentication and authorization practices, confidentiality and privacy policies, customer support provisions, and access to data criteria (Lavery 2010). Similar provisions in cloud computing and hosting licenses include SLAs; security and access provisions; data integrity guarantees; data export and migration support; and confidentiality, privacy, and legal indemnification policies (Zhou et al. 2010).

Although libraries seeking to implement these new data-rich and network-centric services can benefit from being able to look outside traditional in-house IT solutions for hosting and platform support, they often find themselves exchanging one set of complications for another. New factors to be considered when evaluating a cloud-based service provider include security, confidentiality and privacy, legal liability, and organizational stability. Table 1.2 lists each of these categories along with common issues associated with them.

It is important to recognize that these technologies are still in their early stages and are defined more by "best-practice" approaches and less by accepted standards. In addition to NIST, organizations including the Cloud Security Alliance (https://cloudsecurityalliance.org), Open Grid Forum (www.ogf.org), Open Cloud Computing Interface (OCCI; http://occi-wg.org), and Organization for the Advancement of Structured Information Standards (www.oasis-open.org) are working on turning these best-practice approaches into industry standards. At this point libraries are likely to have to make choices with an understanding of the impact proprietary and nonstandard practices will have as they migrate to cloud solutions. Although libraries have historically worked with proprietary systems, the rapid deployment and migration that often accompanies virtualized and cloud services means that adherence to standards and practices that ensure data and

TABLE 1.2
Evaluation of Cloud Computing

Evaluation category	Specific issues
Technology	Platform suitability, control, service stability, required expertise, fit with organizational goals
Security	Adherence to authentication and authorization standards, suitable firewall provisions, fit with local authorization and authentication practices (SAS70, ISO/IEC 27001)
Privacy	Adherence to local, state, and federal regulations; impact of system structure/topography on privacy concerns (HIPPA, FERPA, Patriot Act)
Legal	Domains of legal liability, data ownership provisions, data access provisions
Organizational stability	Risk of organizational stability, structures for handling service in case of organizational failure

service portability, as well as data backup and recovery, are considerations that need to be part of the discussion of cloud and virtualization adoption.

Genres of Cloud-Based or Virtualized Information Services

Cloud computing can be grouped into categories by service type (e.g., SaaS, PaaS, IaaS, DaaS), described using specific features (e.g., subscription, metered, scalable), and used in different deployment models (e.g., public, private, community, hybrid). As our initial exploration of these relationships shows, it can be difficult to compare IT systems from a functional perspective, let alone understand the implications of choosing an IT platform along with a system. In addition, libraries turning to outsourced and hosted solutions need to be prepared to evaluate the technological foundation of those services. Therefore, having a firm understanding of the basic functions of these cloud platforms is crucial in making an informed decision.

Libraries support a wide range of information systems including ILSs, link resolvers, digital asset management systems (DAMS), websites, research guides, internal intranets, and archival information systems. Cloud computing works well for most libraries and library services, but the right balance of platform, deployment environment, and adoption goals naturally drives libraries toward different solutions. It can be difficult to understand how virtualized and cloud services support functional IT needs such as preservation-quality network storage, development and production computing platforms, and acquisition and data management needs. For example, the selection and implementation of archival and digital preservation systems require a consideration of digital object preservation features, network bandwidth, and long-term platform viability. In selecting both a platform and a provider, libraries must be aware of the balance of responsibility that comes with different solutions and be prepared to migrate to new systems in the future. In turning to cloud providers, libraries must also focus on the creation of an efficient and economical cloud infrastructure. In a highly outsourced or SaaS environment, for example, libraries may find that they cannot avoid duplicating resources or overbuying capacity (e.g., paying for extra disk space on multiple platforms or paying support for multiple web service front-end systems). In the coming chapters we explore these issues and see specifically how libraries can both benefit from the advantages and mitigate the risks that come with cloud computing adoption.

REFERENCES

Baev, Simon, Casey Weaver, and Cody Weaver. 2011. "Cost-Efficient Desktop Virtualization Experience at Georgia Southwestern State University." *Journal of Computing Sciences in Colleges* 27 (no. 2): 188–195. http://dl.acm.org/citation.cfm?id=2038836.2038863.

Behrend, Tara S., Eric N. Wiebe, Jennifer E. London, and Emily C. Johnson. 2011. "Cloud Computing Adoption and Usage in Community Colleges." *Behaviour and Information Technology* 30 (no. 2): 231–240. doi:10.1080/0144929X.2010.489118.

Bertot, John. C., Kathryn Sigler, Elizabeth DeCoster, Abigail McDermott, Sarah Katz, Lesley A. Langa, and Justin M. Grimes. 2011. "Public Library Funding and Technology Access Survey: Executive Summary." *Public Libraries and the Internet.* www.plinternetsurvey.org/sites/default/files/publications/2011_plftasexecsummary.pdf.

Blowers, Helene. 2010. "From Realities to Values." *Computers in Libraries* 30 (no. 4): 6–10. www.infotoday.com/cilmag/may10/Blowers.shtml.

Breeding, Marshall. 2011a. "A Cloudy Forecast for Libraries." *Computers in Libraries* 31 (no. 7): 32–34. www.infotoday.com/cilmag/sep11/Breeding.shtml.

———. 2011b. "Library Discovery Services: From the Ground to the Cloud." In *Getting Started with Cloud Computing*, ed. Edward M. Corrado and Heather Lee Moulaison, 71–86. New York: Neal-Schuman.

Fang Liu, Jin Tong, Jian Mao, Robert Bohn, John Messina, Lee Badger, and Dawn Lea. 2011. *NIST Cloud Computing Reference Architecture,* 28. National Institute of Standards and Technology: Washington, DC. www.nist.gov/customcf/get_pdf.cfm?pub_id=909505.

Fitzpatrick, Sean. 2010. "Early Adopters Climb onto OCLC's Web-Scale Management Cloud." *American Libraries* 41 (no. 9): 15.

Gartner. 2011. "Virtualization." Gartner IT Glossary. Gartner Group. www.gartner.com/technology/it-glossary/virtualization.jsp.

Hogan, Michael, Fang Liu, Annie Sokol, and Jin Tong. 2011. *NIST Cloud Computing Standards Roadmap,* 76. National Institute of Standards and Technology: Washington, DC. www.nist.gov/customcf/get_pdf.cfm?pub_id=909024.

Howe, Bill, Garret Cole, Emad Souroush, Paraschos Koutris, Alicia Key, Nodira Khoussainova, and Leilani Battle. 2011. "Database-as-a-Service for Long-Tail Science." *Proceedings of the 23rd International Conference on Scientific and Statistical Database Management,* 480–89. Springer-Verlag: Berlin, Heidelberg. http://dl.acm.org/citation.cfm?id=2032397.2032436.

Hussain, Mohammed, and Hanady Abdulsalam. 2011. "SECaaS: Security as a Service for Cloud-Based Applications." *Proceedings of the Second Kuwait Conference on e-Services and e-Systems*, 8:1–8:4. ACM: New York. doi:10.1145/2107556.2107564.

Kimpton, Michele, and Stu Baker. 2011. "DuraCloud: Preserving the Scholarly Record." Educause National Conference, Philadelphia. http://docs.duraspace.org/documents/DuraCloudEducauseOct2011.pdf.

Krüger, Lars, and Bastian Grabski. 2009. "Using User Context for Accessing IT Resources." *Proceedings of the First International Workshop on Context-Aware Software Technology and Applications,* 33–36. Association for Computing Machinery: New York. doi:10.1145/1595768.1595781.

Lavery, Curtis. 2010. "CDL License Agreement Checklist." California Digital Library, University of California, last modified January 26, 2010. www.cdlib.org/gateways/vendors/checklist.html.

Marko, Kurt. 2012. "Fundamentals: Understanding Private Cloud Stacks." *Information Week Reports*, February 2012. http://reports.informationweek.com/abstract/5/8682/cloud-computing/fundamentals-understanding-private-cloud-stacks.html.

Mell, Peter, and Timothy Grance. 2011. *The NIST Definition of Cloud Computing.* National Institute of Standards and Technology: Washington DC. http://csrc.nist.gov/publications/nistpubs/800-145/SP800-145.pdf.

Metz, Rosalind. 2011. "Understanding the Cloud: An Introduction to the Cloud." In *Getting Started with Cloud Computing*, ed. Edward M. Corrado and Heather Lee Moulaison, 13–27. New York: Neal-Schuman.

Miller, Fred. 2009. "Rationalizing IT Rationing: 10 Ways to Cut the IT Budget (and What Not to Cut)." *EDUCAUSE Quarterly* 32 (no. 2).

Oracle. 2012. "Remote Virtual Machines." In *Oracle VM VirtualBox User Manual.* www.virtualbox.org/manual/ch07.html.

Purdy, Kevin. 2010. "How to Seamlessly Run That One Windows App You Need on a Mac." *Lifehacker*, last modified April 27, 2010. http://lifehacker.com/5521308/how-to-seamlessly-run-that-one-windows-app-you-need-on-a-mac.

Schrier, Robert. A. 2011. "Digital Librarianship Social Media: The Digital Library as Conversation Facilitator." *D-Lib Magazine* 17 (no. 7/8): 1–8. doi:10.1045/july2011-schrier.

Shaffer, Henry E., Samuel F. Averitt, Marc I. Holt, Aaron Peeler, Eric D. Sills, and Mladen A. Vouk. 2009. "NCSU's Virtual Computing Lab: A Cloud Computing Solution." *Computer* 42 (no. 7): 94–97. doi:10.1109/MC.2009.230.

Smith, David M. 2010. "Hype Cycle for Cloud Computing, 2010." Gartner. www.gartner.com/DisplayDocument?doc_cd=201557.

Smith, James E., and Ravi Nair. 2005. "The Architecture of Virtual Machines." *Computer* 38 (no. 5): 32–38. doi:10.1109/MC.2005.173.

Thomas, Stan. J., and Paul M. Whitener. 2010. "In the Zone: Virtual Computing on a Budget." *Proceedings of the 41st ACM Technical Symposium on Computer Science Education*, 366–70. http://portal.acm.org/citation.cfm?id=1734388.

Wong, Danny. 2008. "Kickin' It Old School! Dealing with Legacy Applications." *Proceedings of the 36th Annual ACM SIGUCCS Fall Conference: Moving Mountains, Blazing Trails,* New York, 55–58. doi:10.1145/1449956.1449975.

Zambare, Aparna, Anne Marie Casey, John Fierst, David Ginsburg, Judith O'Dell, and Timothy Peters. 2009. "Assuring Access: One Library's Journey from Print to Electronic Only Subscriptions." *Serials Review* 35 (no. 2): 70–74. doi:10.1016/j.serrev.2009.03.002.

Zhou, Minqi, Rong Zhang, Wei Xie, Weining Qian, and Aoying Zhou. 2010. "Security and Privacy in Cloud Computing: A Survey." *Sixth International Conference on Semantics Knowledge and Grids*, Beijing, 105–12. doi:10.1109/SKG.2010.19.

Chapter Two

The Landscape of Cloud Computing and Virtualization Adoption

Libraries are at a crossroads in IT adoption because of rapid changes in purchasing, collection development, information management, and public service expectations (Attis et al. 2012). These changes have been accompanied by changing approaches to metadata standards, authority control, and information management systems (Seikel and Steele 2011). The shift in IT environments has included the proliferation of systems for different services (e.g., digital reference, resource management, digital libraries) and an emergence of new vendor and open-source community services that are virtualized, hosted, or cloud-based (Breeding 2011). In particular, LIS vendors are redefining their services to leverage cloud computing in the "next-generation" of LIS systems. In addition to the vendor-driven shift of the ILS to the cloud, libraries are turning to cloud computing to address a wider range of information system needs.

Much of the research in library adoption of cloud computing focuses on specific uses or platforms. For example, Malpas (2011) explored the role of cloud computing in large-scale digital text collections and Schonfeld and Housewright (2010) explored the impact of "network-scale" learning and resource use on academic teaching and scholarship. Both studies found a growing reliance on network-based technologies and Internet-accessible digital text collections by both academic libraries and their constituents. Some research has focused on how to incorporate cloud computing into IT planning (Reeves 2010), and academic institutions are increasingly incorporating virtualized technologies in strategic plans (Furman University 2011). In addition to organization-focused studies, other research is finding that library patrons including students in academic environments and the general public are increasingly adopting cloud-based, social, and mobile information technologies (Anderson and Rainie 2010; Smith 2010). These studies highlight issues of perceived value, organizational impact, and environmental influence in relation to cloud computing adoption. At the same time, they highlight many of the challenges associated with this process including technical, legal, operational, and financial pressures.

Although there have been several library IT adoption surveys, including Breeding's research on library automation systems (www.librarytechnology.org), there has been little research that examines virtualized and cloud computing adoption across the range of library IT services. On the basis of a survey conducted in 2011, this chapter seeks to close this gap and identify factors that influence cloud adoption.

SURVEY FRAMEWORK

Understanding the factors that enable and inhibit IT change can be an important element of change management and can facilitate the exploration of tools and their fit with your library. There are several ways to approach this discussion, but two models in particular inform organizational understanding of technology adoption: the "technology acceptance model" (TAM; Davis 1989) and the "technology, organization and environments model" (TOE; Tornatzky et al. 1990). These models provide frameworks for understanding the relationship between technologies and their use by individuals or organizations. Another model often used in technology adoption studies is "diffusion of innovation theory" (Rogers 2003), which explores technology adoption by examining factors including advantage, compatibility with other systems, and system complexity and focuses on qualifying adoption patterns. In contrast, the TOE and TAM models explore factors that influence technology adoption and more directly speak to the types of organizational decision making that are key in library IT decisions.

These models take somewhat different approaches to understanding technology adoption. The TAM model explores the natural tension between the perceived usefulness and ease of use of technologies. In contrast to TAM's perception-based model, the TOE model examines various contexts that influence technology adoption (e.g., organizational and environmental). These two perspectives help shed light on factors that influence individual and organizational assessment of the value of technologies (e.g., ease of use, perceived value, social context, organizational values). Specifically, the TAM model provides a structure for understanding the individual, social, and technological context surrounding technology adoption. In contrast, the TOE model provides a framework for understanding the interaction of organizational, technological, and external (to the organization) factors.

Previous studies have also used these models to explore cloud adoption in educational and technology environments. For example, the TAM model has been used to examine the factors that influence cloud computing adoption in community college systems (Behrend et al. 2011), and the TOE model has been used to explore the organizational factors that influence the adoption of technology in different contexts (Daylami et al. 2005). The inclusion of both models helps frame the research in terms of the participant's perceptions of cloud computing and situates their use of cloud computing within the organization. The analysis of survey responses looked for elements of each model, including personal views of ease of use/value (i.e., TAM) and personal views of environmental, organizational, and technical factors (i.e., TOE) in relation to four computing platforms. Figure 2.1 shows the coding framework that was used in this survey.

	Non-virtualized	Internal/ private cloud virtualized	Public/ community cloud virtualized	Outsourced
Personal views (e.g., perceived value, ease of use)				
Environmental influence (e.g., industry support, professional standards, community needs)				
Organizational influence (e.g., privacy, legal, financial perspective, staff expertise, service focus)				
Technical influence (e.g., technical capacity to address service need, technical fit with organizational goals)				

FIGURE 2.1

Framework of factors influencing cloud computing adoption

Figure 2.1 includes four categories of virtualized/cloud computing that were created using the NIST model. These four models (nonvirtualized, internal noncloud or private cloud virtualization, public or community cloud virtualization, and outsourced) represent a mix of deployment contexts (e.g., public, community, private) and service models (SaaS, PaaS, IaaS) and were selected because they have common real-world examples in library IT environments.

One of the challenges with this study framework was finding a suitable way to categorize cloud platforms that made sense to a large population of participants. Although the study focused on library IT personnel, the population surveyed included a mix of highly technical and nontechnical librarians. To control for this variation, the categories were informally tested with technical and nontechnical librarians and refined to be as understandable as possible. In this study framework, *nonvirtualized* refers to traditional library IT systems that run on dedicated hardware within the organization. In contrast, *internally virtualized or private cloud* refers to IT systems that are run within the organization but use a specific form of virtualization. It is important to differentiate the virtualization of multiple machines on a single hardware stack (virtualization) from a new range of software platforms that "unify server, storage and network resources into a common resource pool" (Marko 2012, 4). The study grouped external cloud computing adoption into two genres, "public/community cloud" and "outsourced." In category testing with librarians the term *outsourced*, though not truly representative of the SaaS technical concept, was more representative of the form of SaaS solutions adopted by libraries and was a commonly understood concept among nontechnical librarians. Table 2.1 provides detailed explanations of each platform. Although conflating service

TABLE 2.1
Cloud Computing/Virtualization Adoption Platforms

Implementation type	Type of system
Virtualized using in-house systems	PaaS or IaaS in a private cloud environment
Virtualized using cloud resources run by library IT	PaaS or IaaS in a public or community cloud environment
Outsourced to external providers	Outsourced solutions described primarily as SaaS cloud solutions
Run in-house (not virtualized)	IT system run on dedicated hardware in a nonvirtualized configuration
Not supported at my library	

models and deployment contexts poses challenges for an in-depth understanding of library adoption of cloud computing, it allowed wider participation and enabled the study to focus on common real-world uses of cloud and virtualized technologies.

Three research questions examined the adoption of cloud computing and virtualization in libraries and explored the factors IT librarians consider when evaluating these technologies and their use in libraries:

- What is the landscape and state of cloud computing and virtualized technology adoption in libraries? What services are libraries providing using cloud- and virtual-based platforms? What types of cloud- and virtual-based platforms are being used in libraries?
- What enabling and inhibiting factors are identified by librarians in relation to the adoption of cloud computing?
- What actions would enhance the adoption of cloud computing in libraries? How could these actions be designed or implemented?

METHODS

The study was designed and administered using an online survey platform (see www.alaeditions.org/webextras for the full survey). Participants were solicited from a range of library IT discussion boards including Code4Lib, Lita-L, SYSLIB-L, and WEB4LIB. The total number of participating libraries was 111. Participants answered a range of questions including demographic information on library size and focus, questions about the implementation of information services (e.g., ILS and OpenURL resolver), and motivations/concerns regarding cloud computing adoption. Survey data was analyzed to discover common themes using the framework represented in figure 2.1.

A mixed-method approach was valuable in this study because it provided both baseline descriptive data on the state of cloud computing and virtualized technology adoption in libraries and higher-level data surrounding the subjective motivations and enabling/inhibiting factors for librarians making decisions about technology adoption. The survey included quantitative data on the type of services provided by libraries using cloud platforms and qualitative data on the enabling and inhibiting factors related to decision making in IT for libraries. Participants were asked to categorize their library's use of cloud and virtualized technologies and reflect on technical issues, economic factors, and organizational factors that enabled or inhibited cloud adoption. In total, fourteen categories of library systems were evaluated:

1. Digital asset management system (DAMS, e.g., DSpace, Fedora, CONTENTdm)
2. Discovery service (e.g., Summon, Primo, Encore)
3. Electronic resource management system
4. Electronic reserves systems
5. Interlibrary loan system
6. Integrated library system (ILS)
7. Library patron client computers
8. Library staff client computers
9. Library servers
10. Library website
11. OPAC/discovery layer (for books, media, serials)
12. OpenURL resolver
13. Research guides
14. Staff intranet

Participants were also given the option of including additional system classes. Based on their selections of one of the four virtualization categories for system types in general, participants were asked to comment on enabling and inhibiting factors that influenced their selection. Participants were not asked specifically about systems but rather generally (e.g., "You indicated that some services operate in an internally virtualized environment…").

RESULTS

In total, the survey received 111 responses. All questions in the survey were optional, so response totals for each question may differ. The survey data were grouped into three main areas: demographic information, quantitative results on cloud computing adoption, and qualitative results on cloud computing adoption.

Survey data were coded with guidance from the framework represented in figure 2.1 but were open to addition and interpretation based on participant-generated themes. Coding focused on identifying themes and constructs that influence adoption of cloud computing and virtualized technologies. Codes were refined and contributed to the development of an expanded framework focused on the exploration of factors and constructs important in considering new IT services. Quantitative data were analyzed to provide both descriptive statistics on cloud computing adoption and inferential statistics on relationships between institution type and size, service type (e.g., digital library, reference service), and technology platform adopted (e.g., cloud, virtualized, traditional).

Demographics

The majority of libraries that responded to the survey were academic (n=57). Other libraries included public (n=13) and law or medical (n=7). Of note, six participants represented consortial IT support for libraries, and there were libraries that served multiple populations including academic/public (n=2) and academic/medical (n=1). The low number of responses from nonacademic libraries limits generalizability of these findings. In fact, the demographics point to a study population dominated by medium-sized academic institutions, and the organizational and environmental issues raised should be considered within that context.

A majority of respondents also indicated that their libraries have relatively small environments of one to three IT support staff (n=47). The overall size of library staff showed a more equal distribution, with an emphasis on slightly small and medium-sized libraries (29.9 percent with 40 or fewer staff) versus large (14.9 percent with 41–119 staff) and very large (19.4 percent with 120 or more staff). Patron population size varied, with over 32 percent of respondents serving 15,000 or more patrons and 22.4 percent of libraries serving between 3,000 and 15,000 patrons. There was also a mix of branch sizes, with 27 percent (n=37) of respondents supporting a single library branch and 21 percent (n=29) supporting two to five branches. The number of participants supporting larger branch organizations was much smaller (6–20 branches, n=13; 21–30 branches, n=4; 31 or more, n=8).

State of Adoption of Cloud Services for Library IT Services

The survey found a variety of adoption rates and adoption platforms for each system. In some cases (e.g., ILS), adoption trended toward nonvirtualized solutions; in others (e.g., research guides), internally and externally virtualized/cloud solutions predominated. Table 2.2 shows the various adoption rates of each platform/system. Tables 2.3 and 2.4 group systems by platform based on frequency of adoption. Table 2.3 shows service/platform groupings used by 20 percent or more of participants.

TABLE 2.2
Adoption Rates of Selected Systems (%)

	ERMS	Discovery	ILS	Website	OpenURL	Research guides
I don't know	4	3	1	3	5	4
No option applicable	13	13	7	4	8	8
No response	18	16	15	15	16	16
Not supported at my library	16	30	1	1	12	13
Outsourced to external providers	19	24	14	8	32	28
Run in-house (not virtualized)	19	3	42	31	18	20
Virtualized using cloud resources run by library IT	4	3	9	8	3	4
Virtualized using in-house systems	5	8	12	30	5	7

TABLE 2.3
System Implementation Type: >20% of Libraries

Implementation type	Systems
Nonvirtualized	e-reserves, electronic resource management system, interlibrary loan, ILS, client computers, staff computers, website, OPAC, intranet, OpenURL, research guides
Virtualized using in-house resources	website, OPAC
Virtualized using external cloud resources	
Outsourced	discovery service, electronic resource management system, interlibrary loan, OpenURL, research guides

TABLE 2.4
System Implementation Type: 10–19.9% of Libraries

Implementation type	Systems
Nonvirtualized	
Virtualized using in-house resources	e-reserves, interlibrary loan, ILS, client computers, staff computers, intranet
Virtualized using external cloud resources	ILS, OPAC
Outsourced	e-reserves, ILS, OPAC

Table 2.4 shows service/platform groupings used by 10–19 percent of participants. Services are listed multiple times (e.g., website) if their adoption rate met the range associated with the table in multiple categories.

These adoption levels indicate some common trends in the libraries surveyed. For example, older systems such as ILS and library OPACs tended to be both widely adopted and run only in a nonvirtualized environment. Likewise, client computing tended to be nonvirtualized (e.g., public client computers and staff client computers), but there were instances of desktop virtualization for both client and staff solutions. In contrast, more recently developed systems (e.g., discovery services) and datacentric systems (e.g., OpenURL resolvers) tended to be virtualized using in-house or external cloud systems or outsourced completely. For example, Table 2.2 shows that 24 percent of respondents ran a discovery service as an outsourced service, an additional 11 percent ran the service using some form of virtualized or cloud platform, and 3 percent indicated that these services were run as a nonvirtualized service. Although several systems grouped around nonvirtualized and outsourced solutions, it was interesting to note that the only service that showed a substantial locally or cloud-based (but not outsourced) virtualized solution was the library website (31 percent).

As table 2.3 shows, some systems fit into multiple implementation platforms. For example, both OPAC and library website systems fit under both internally virtualized and nonvirtualized platforms. It is interesting that this view of the data shows a grouping of systems under either nonvirtualized or outsourced solutions. This gap in adoption points to an interesting trend in cloud adoption toward outsourced solutions. Table 2.4, which shows that fewer libraries use internal and external virtual/cloud systems, supports this trend and indicates that libraries less frequently adopt internal virtualization and external PaaS/IaaS cloud solutions as compared to nonvirtualized or SaaS solutions. The lack of use of externally virtualized (e.g., PaaS or IaaS) services raises questions about the factors that influence library adoption of technology platforms and could have a considerable impact on the development of new library systems (particularly open-source solutions) in the coming years.

A second trend in the data is the prevalence of data-intensive and new genres of systems in the outsourced category while traditional systems (e.g., the ILS) remain nonvirtualized. Participant responses regarding the motivations for implementing systems in nonvirtualized environments indicate that libraries are shifting these systems toward cloud-based solutions but are still considering options or have yet to find cloud solutions that meet all of their needs. The ILS is the most representative system of this type, seeing relatively low levels of implementation in each of the three virtualized categories, with 14 percent of libraries reported using an ILS on a virtualized platform, 10 percent using some form of external cloud provider, and just over 16 percent using an outsourced or SaaS solution. Though individual approaches showed relatively low percentages, it is worth noting that over 40 percent of libraries had turned to some internally or externally virtualized solution. This trend was seen across most systems. When grouped into virtualized and nonvirtualized solutions, it was common, with the exception of client computing, to see a relatively high level of virtualized use. This trend included server virtualization as well, with 41 percent of libraries using internally virtualized resources.

Perceptions of Cloud Computing and Virtualization

In addition to exploring the landscape of cloud computing adoption, the survey also explored the participants' view of the potential impact of cloud computing and virtualization. Participants were asked to indicate their agreement with two statements about both cloud computing and virtualization: "Cloud computing/virtualization is a current priority of the administration," and "Cloud computing/virtualization has the potential to transform library IT in the short term." Figures 2.2 through 2.5 show participant responses for these questions.

The data from these questions show a largely positive view of the impact of both cloud computing and virtualization. Likewise, survey participants largely viewed cloud computing and virtualization as priorities of the administration. There was some variation in participant views of the priority of cloud computing and virtualization, indicating that participants are bullish on cloud computing and virtualization but more positive about the latter.

Motivating and Inhibiting Factors of Cloud Computing and Virtualization

The survey also collected qualitative data on the motivating and inhibiting factors related to the use of cloud computing and virtualization resources. For each series of qualitative responses, codes were generated from responses and then mapped onto the survey analysis framework. Statements were coded into TAM areas (value and ease of use) when the participant stated a perception (e.g., nonvirtual is easier) as opposed to a situation (e.g., current IT policy inhibits cloud migration).

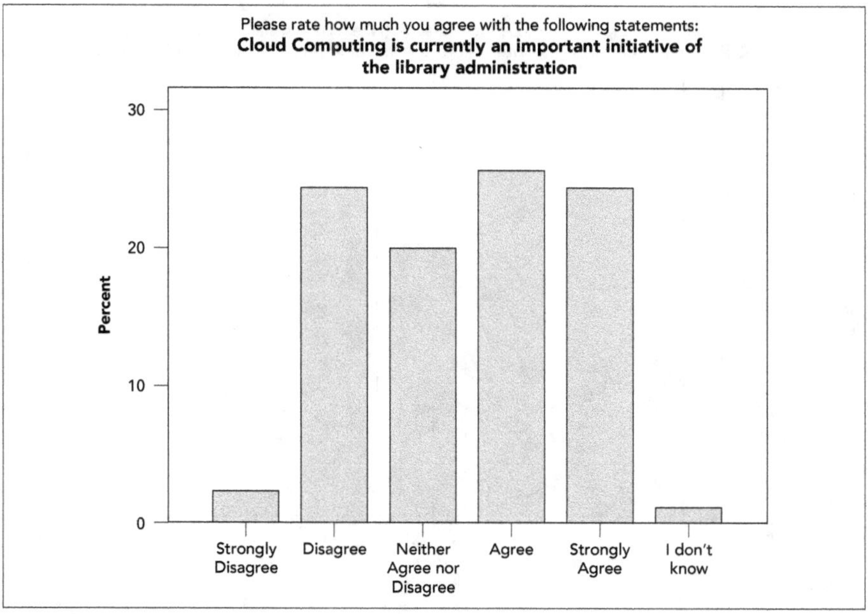

FIGURE 2.2
Cloud computing is a priority

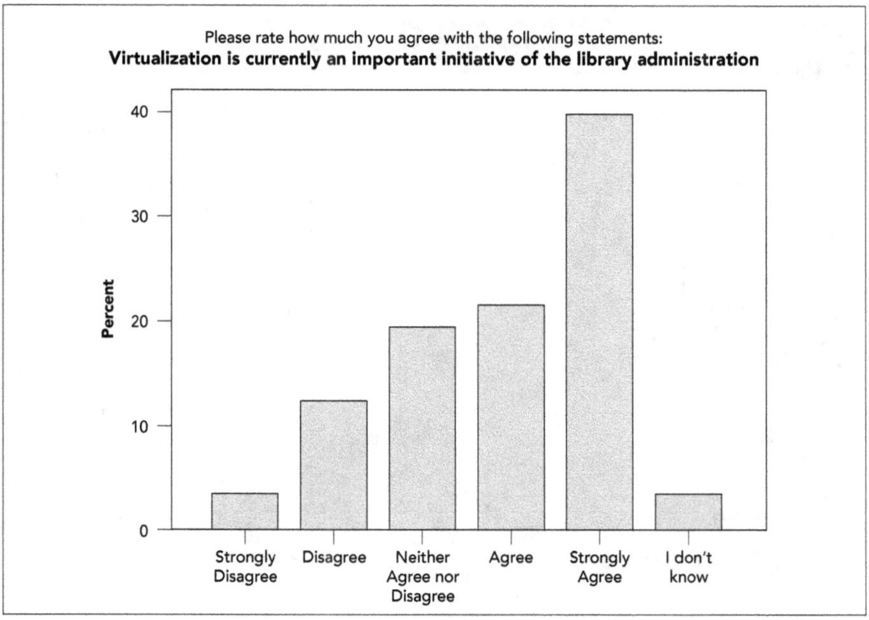

FIGURE 2.3
Virtualization is a priority

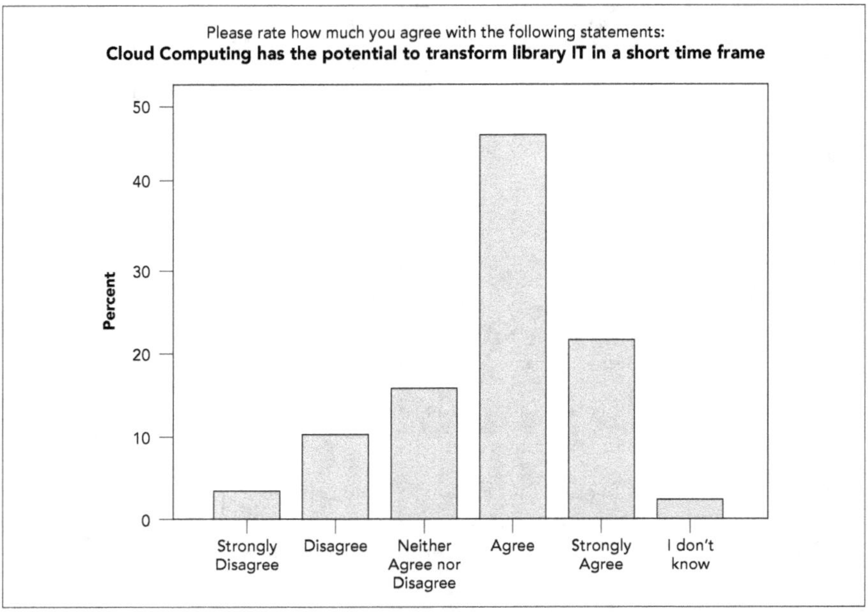

FIGURE 2.4

Cloud computing can transform IT

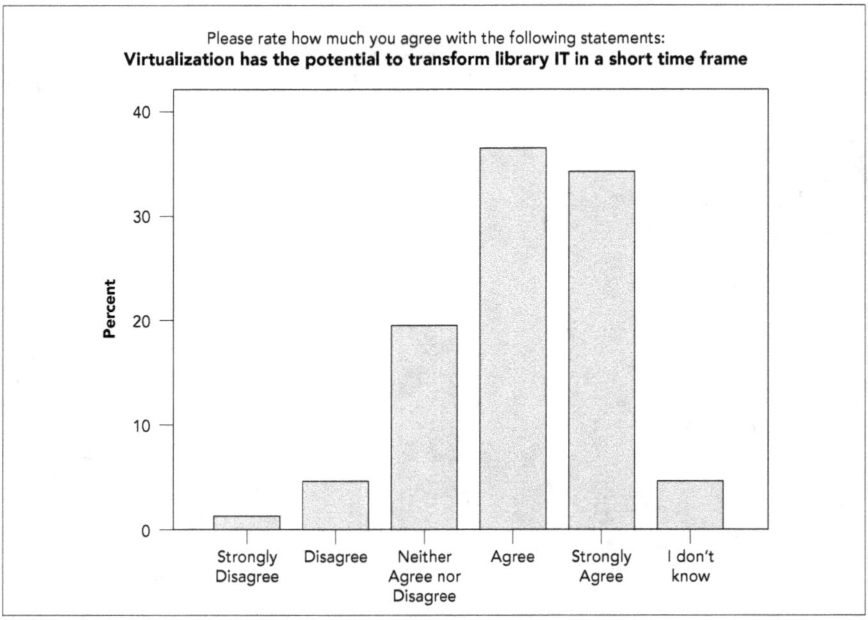

FIGURE 2.5

Virtualization can transform IT

Many cases overlapped (e.g., cost-benefit analysis, lack of knowledge/expertise), particularly where these statements appeared to influence a judgment about the value or ease of use of virtualized solutions.

Responses were coded for theme and type of platform referenced and coded for positive, neutral, or negative perspectives. In total, 168 factors grouped into thirty-one distinct themes related to cloud computing adoption were identified. Qualitative themes tended to focus more on technical, organizational, or environmental statements (seventeen themes) as opposed to perceived value or ease-of-use statements (ten themes). Of the latter, only two themes explicitly addressed ease of use and all other cases focused on issues surrounding perceived value. In contrast, each element of the TOE model was associated with several themes.

Table 2.5 lists each code and the percentage of occurrence. The most commonly used themes were "cost-benefit analysis" (19 percent) and "technology supports IT service productivity, efficiency, flexibility, scalability" (19 percent). These themes were always mentioned in a positive manner but not always about the same type of cloud platform. All three virtualized or cloud computing adoption platforms were cited as being advantageous from a cost-benefit perspective. In contrast, the theme "technology supports IT service productivity" was mentioned only in reference to virtualization and outsourced platforms.

Themes such as "adherence to vendor specifications," "legacy systems inhibit migration," and "library in middle of IT investment cycle" were listed as reasons why certain platforms had been adopted or not adopted. "Adherence to vendor specifications" was characterized both positively and negatively but tended to associate positive views with cloud computing platforms and negative views with nonvirtualized platforms. There were instances of neutral comments in this area, too, indicating that some participants viewed system requirements, as opposed to technical requirements or system infrastructure, as a driving factor. This view seems to be in contrast with themes such as "technology enables service that could not be run locally" and "platform supports higher quality IT service support," both of which were always positive and always focused on virtualized or outsourced platforms.

Table 2.6 groups identified themes using the TOE model. Although all three areas (environment, organization, and technology) have a variety of associated themes, organizational themes were the most prevalent. The two most common themes were associated with organizational influences (e.g., cost-benefit analysis) and technical influences (e.g., technology supports IT service productivity, efficiency, flexibility, scalability). For each of the areas there was a mix of positive and negative views. For example, the presence of a cost-benefit perspective as both

TABLE 2.5

Qualitative Adoption Themes and Frequency

Code	% Occurrence
Cost-benefit analysis	19.16
Technology supports IT service productivity, efficiency, flexibility, scalability	19.16
Legacy systems inhibit adoption	6.59
Adherence to vendor specifications	5.39
Library in middle of IT investment cycle	4.19
Technology enables services that could not be run locally (IT capacity)	3.59
Technology is tuned for specialized use	3.59
Technology mandated by organizational IT	3.59
Current IT policy, politics inhibits cloud migration	2.99
Limited IT resources inhibit migration	2.99
Platform supports higher quality IT service support (e.g., SLA) and assessment	2.99
Concerns over liability associated with platform (legal, privacy, security)	2.40
Lack of knowledge/expertise	2.40
Technology enables services not supported by parent IT organization	2.40
Technology adopted fits service	1.80
Technology enables exploration in capacity and troubleshooting	1.80
Technology facilitates collaboration with organizational IT	1.80
Lack of cloud or virtualized infrastructure	1.20
Measured adoption based on state of market	1.20
No local support for virtualization	1.20
Processing limitations of cloud	1.20
Security infrastructure inhibits virtualized or cloud adoption	1.20
System backup requirements inhibit cloud migration	1.20
Technology adoption is required for community participation	1.20
Technology inhibits customization	1.20
Bandwidth limitations of cloud	0.60
Business continuity	0.60
Platform is easier to use	0.60
SaaS lock into vendor is bad but easier to manage	0.60
Technology is a bridge to other services	0.60
Technology is not needed	0.60

TABLE 2.6
Qualitative Themes Grouped Using the TOE Model

TOE element	Example codes
Environmental influence	Adherence to vendor specifications Lack of cloud or virtualized infrastructure Measured adoption based on state of market SaaS lock-in with vendor is bad but easier to manage Technology adoption is required for community participation
Organizational influence	Business continuity Concerns over liability associated with platform Cost-benefit analysis Current IT policy, politics inhibits cloud migration Lack of knowledge/expertise Library in middle of IT investment cycle Limited IT resources inhibit migration No local support for virtualization Platform supports higher-quality IT service Technology enables services not supported by parent IT organization Technology enables services that could not be run locally Technology facilitates collaboration with organizational IT Technology is not needed Technology mandated by organizational IT
Technical influence	Bandwidth limitations of cloud Legacy systems inhibit adoption Platform is easier to use Processing limitations of cloud Security infrastructure inhibits virtualized or cloud adoption Technology adopted fits service Technology enables exploration in capacity and troubleshooting Technology inhibits customization Technology is a bridge to other services Technology is tuned for specialized use Technology supports IT service productivity, efficiency, flexibility, scalability

positive and negative among the platform types indicates that libraries are highly cost conscious when making IT service selections. There was also variation in how libraries used these platforms to either connect with or distance themselves from organizational IT. These issues appear to have little to do with the benefits or drawbacks of the platform itself and more to do with the internal operations of these organizations.

MODEL FOR EVALUATING VIRTUALIZED TECHNOLOGY ADOPTION IN LIBRARIES

Our data show that libraries are using cloud and virtualized platforms in different ways, but that overall the view of these technologies is positive. Whereas our review of literature found a wide range of issues one should consider when moving to an internally or externally sourced virtual solution, participants in this study focused on issues of vendor compliance, cost-benefit analysis, and positive impacts of cloud computing on efficiency and flexibility rather than on security, business continuity, privacy, or liability. Likewise, the high frequency of libraries citing a positive view of virtualization and cloud platforms but expressing hesitancy given current local IT infrastructure points to a real need for library and perhaps organizational IT departments to expand their capacity to support cloud-based services. Some other common barriers to cloud adoption included the presence of legacy systems, vendor requirements that prevent virtualization or cloud adoption, internal organizational issues, current investment in technology, and lack of expertise. Despite these inhibiting factors, primary motivations tended to be perceived improvement in service, interest in resource (cost, staff time) efficiency, and interest in new services. These factors could prove to be good measures of whether a cloud or virtualized platform is a good fit for a given service and could certainly help libraries make educated decisions about the potential advantage or liability of cloud choices.

Perhaps the most difficult part of moving to any IT solution is understanding how to weigh the positive and negative issues surrounding a platform. Some participants used their qualitative response to discuss a decision process or compare issues in this manner. For example, one library recognized the risk of vendor lock-in when moving to SaaS platforms but indicated that service efficiency outweighed the risk. Likewise, several libraries indicated interest in migrating but were moving slowly to be sure that they adopted a platform only after the market had tested its viability. Despite some rich exploration of organizational and environmental issues, there was little discussion of the roles of networked data, open data, or open-source software in making IT decisions. Likewise, security and privacy issues, though often represented as key concerns in the literature (Grant 2011, 47; Velte et al. 2009, 35), were not discussed at the same level of specificity as technical and organizational issues. This emphasis may well be due to the population or the style of the questions, but it raises a good question about professional perceptions of legal, policy, and security concerns in virtualized and cloud computing environments.

Although the primary goal of this research was to help identify a model that libraries could use to evaluate their own level of cloud adoption and consider the factors that are influencing their IT decisions, it is worth comparing our results with other cloud computing adoption studies. For example, a 2011 study by the Aberdeen Group found that among cloud adopters 68 percent had turned to private cloud and internal virtualization services and 50 percent had turned to SaaS solutions (Brink 2011, 2). Like Brink's study, the research presented in this chapter also found higher rates of private cloud and SaaS adoption and much lower rates of PaaS (22 percent) and IaaS (31 percent) adoption. Overall, Brink found much higher overall adoption of cloud computing (81 percent) than was found in published studies that included assessment of library cloud computing use. For example, the Library Resource Guide report on funding priorities in libraries found an overall cloud computing adoption level of 7 percent in libraries in 2011 and 12 percent in 2012 (McKendrick 2012). In contrast, we found an adoption rate over 90 percent.

The Library Resource Guide survey also found that libraries were tending not to turn to IT as a means for saving money; only 13 percent of respondents indicated that they would reduce IT expenditures in 2011 and 11 percent in 2012. Similarly, that study found that only 1 percent of libraries were planning to increase spending on cloud computing in the coming year (McKendrick 2012, 11, 15).

The variation between findings, at the least, points to a need for more formal study of cloud computing adoption rates. The results may also indicate a gap between library views of cloud computing and their movement in funding cloud initiatives.

Our study did not focus on patron service requirements, but they may help explain why libraries are moving to new IT platforms. For example, the Public Library Funding and Technology Access Survey of 2010 reported expanded interest in a wide range of digital services including technology training, e-government services, licensed electronic resources, and digital reference services (Bertot et al. 2011). Bertot and colleagues also found considerable increases in library IT service use in the previous year including public workstations, Wi-Fi, electronic collections, and training. This gap between patron demand demonstrated by Bertot and the allocation of resources discussed by McKendrick indicates that there may be room for libraries to leverage cloud computing and virtualization platforms to save resources and improve services.

CONCLUSION

This survey of virtualization, cloud computing, and outsourcing adoption in libraries both underscores the current interest in cloud computing and virtualization and demonstrates which views are prevalent among adopters. The gaps found between library and IT literature and survey participants indicate that the questions about cloud computing and virtualization may be different for different audiences or perhaps are shifting as cloud computing matures. The survey also demonstrates a growing reliance on outsourced library IT as opposed to PaaS or IaaS approaches and indicates a slow but growing trend to migrate older and core library systems (e.g., the ILS) to these environments. These survey results should not be overgeneralized, but the evaluative model represented in figure 2.1 and the grouped themes presented in tables 2.4 and 2.5 may help libraries understand their own IT environment in more detail.

REFERENCES

Anderson, Janna, and Lee Rainie. 2010. "The Future of Cloud Computing." Pew Internet Trust Report, June 11, 2010. http://pewinternet.org/Reports/2010/The-future-of-cloud-computing.aspx.

Attis, David, Colin Koprosk, Chris Mille, Kevin Matovich, and Hillary Tisdal. 2012. *Redefining the Academic Library: Managing the Migration to Digital Information Services.* University Library Council. www.educationadvisoryboard.com/pdf/23634-EAB-Redefining-the-Academic-Library.pdf.

Behrend, Tara S., Eric N. Wiebe, Jennifer E. London, and Emily C. Johnson. 2011. "Cloud Computing Adoption and Usage in Community Colleges." *Behaviour and Information Technology* 30 (no. 2): 231–40. doi:10.1080/0144929X.2010.489118.

Bertot, John. C., Kathryn Sigler, Elizabeth DeCoster, Abigail McDermott, Sarah Katz, Lesley A. Langa, and Justin M. Grimes. 2011. "Public Library Funding and Technology Access Survey: Executive Summary." *Public Libraries and the Internet.* www.plinternetsurvey.org/sites/default/files/publications/2011_plftasexecsummary.pdf.

Breeding, Marshall. 2011. "A Cloudy Forecast for Libraries." *Computers in Libraries* 31 (no. 7): 32–34. www.infotoday.com/cilmag/sep11/Breeding.shtml.

Brink, Derek E. 2011. "Security and Cloud: Augment, or Abdicate?" Aberdeen Group. http://resources.idgenterprise.com/original/AST-0054287_rp-aberdeen-security-cloud.pdf.

Davis, Fred. D. 1989. "Perceived Usefulness, Perceived Ease of Use, and User Acceptance of Information Technology." *MIS Quarterly* 13 (no. 3): 319–40. doi:10.2307/249008.

Daylami, Nozar, Terry Ryan, Lorne Olfman, and Conrad Shayo. 2005. "Determinants of Application Service Provider (ASP) Adoption as an Innovation." *Proceedings of the 38th Annual Hawaii International Conference on System Sciences*. doi:10.1109/HICSS.2005.193.

Furman University. 2011. "A Strategic Plan for Furman University Information Technology." www2.furman.edu/sites/ITS/About/Documents/IT_Strategic_Plan_final_public.pdf.

Grant, Carl. 2011. "Head in the Clouds? A Librarian/Vendor Perspective on Cloud Computing." In *Getting Started with Cloud Computing*, ed. Edward M. Corrado and Heather Lee Moulaison, 71–86. New York: Neal-Schuman.

Malpas, Constance. 2011. "Cloud-Sourcing Research Collections: Managing Print in the Mass-Digitized Library Environment." OCLC Research. www.oclc.org/research/publications/library/2011/2011-01.pdf.

Marko, Kurt. 2012. "Fundamentals: Understanding Private Cloud Stacks." *Information Week Reports*, February 2012. http://reports.informationweek.com/abstract/5/8682/cloud-computing/fundamentals-understanding-private-cloud-stacks.html.

McKendrick, Joseph. 2012. "The Digital Squeeze: Libraries at the Crossroads—The Library Resource Guide Benchmark Study on 2012 Library Spending Plans." Unisphere Research. www.libraryresource.com/downloads/researchreports.

Mitchell, Erik. 2011. "What Cloud Computing Means for Libraries. In *Getting Started with Cloud Computing*, ed. Edward M. Corrado and Heather Lee Moulaison, 37–44. New York: Neal-Schuman.

Ovadia, Steven. 2010. "Navigating the Challenges of the Cloud." *Behavioral and Social Science Librarian* 19 (no. 3): 233–36. doi:10.1080/01639269.2010.498764.

Reeves, Drue. 2010. "Managing Availability and Performance Risks in the Cloud: Expect the Unexpected." *ECAR REPORT*, 1–33, last modified December 7, 2010. www.educause.edu/Resources/ManagingAvailabilityandPerform/219309.

Rogers, Everett. M. 2003. *Diffusion of Innovations*. New York: Simon and Schuster.

Schiller, Kurt. 2011. "Amazon EC2 Outage Highlights Risks." *Information Today* 28 (no. 6): 10. www.infotoday.com/IT/jun11/index.shtml.

Schonfeld, Roger. C., and Ross Housewright. 2010. "Faculty Survey 2009: Key Strategic Insights for Libraries, Publishers, and Societies." Ithaka S+R. www.sr.ithaka.org/research-publications/faculty-survey-2009.

Seikel, Michele, and Thomas Steele. 2011. "How MARC Has Changed: The History of the Format and Its Forthcoming Relationship to RDA." *Technical Services Quarterly* 28 (no. 3): 322–34. doi:10.1080/07317131.2011.574519.

Smith, David. M. 2010. "Hype Cycle for Cloud Computing, 2010." Gartner. www.gartner.com/DisplayDocument?doc_cd=201557.

Tornatzky, Lois. G., Mitchell Fleischer, and Alok Chakrabarti. 1990. *The Processes of Technological Innovation*. Lexington MA: D.C. Heath.

Velte, Anthony. T., Toby J. Velte, and Robert Elsenpeter. 2009. *Cloud Computing: A Practical Approach*. New York: McGraw-Hill.

Chapter Three

Selecting and Implementing Solutions

In this chapter we look at technical, organizational, legal, and staffing/expertise issues in more detail and consider library-specific factors that influence adoption of cloud-based services. This examination is based on the responses of participants in the chapter 2 survey, on approaches described in the literature on cloud computing (e.g., Reese 2009; Rittinghouse and Ransome 2009), and on case studies of library adoption of cloud computing and virtualization (Fox 2009; Han 2010; Mitchell 2010).

Our survey found variation in cloud computing adoption rates and different motivating and inhibiting factors with regards to organizational issues, technical/functional requirements, and perceived benefits. This points to the likelihood that there is not a "one-size-fits-all" solution for cloud computing in libraries but rather a need to find the best fit for each institution. Although it was difficult to compare the context of cloud adoption between libraries and other information organizations, there was a clear emphasis on privately virtualized or completely outsourced (e.g., SaaS) approaches in both our survey and other research reported in chapter 2. There were common themes mentioned that contextualized this trend, including lack of IT support or local expertise and concerns over the ability to sustain complex IT systems. These concerns are significant given the fact that as libraries are adopting new information services they are often faced with choices that require distinguishing between cloud, virtualized, and traditional IT approaches. Breeding's (2011) work in particular has focused on this issue in regards to the ILS. He found not only a continued shift toward cloud solutions using

SaaS and PaaS platforms but also a reenvisioning of the structure of these systems including changing approaches to bibliographic and other data management and a focus on data and service interoperability. In evaluating these systems libraries must understand both the IT service and functional implications of their decisions. In addition, as libraries adopt or migrate to cloud-based platforms, new issues such as service quality and service-level agreements (SLAs) and new takes on traditional issues such as vendor lock-in and system functionality need to be considered.

One goal of this book is to give librarians the tools they need to assess and compare cloud, virtualized, and nonvirtualized IT environments. By having a strong understanding of the types of virtualization and cloud computing that are available along with the required support services that come with these platforms, librarians are better prepared to make well-informed system selections. This chapter focuses on issues related to technology adoption as opposed to system functionality, but the latter is a very real concern as well. In weighing the technical differences between systems and organizational/environmental factors it is also worth considering the relationships between organizational units, IT systems, IT services, and end-user information needs. In IT service environments, for example, there is considerable focus on the relationships between capacity (both technical and organizational), risk management, and service or end-user goals (Addy 2007, 45). Libraries should not assume that their view of these elements, or even their definition, is identical to their counterparts' in organizational IT. Schaffhauser (2010) observes that libraries define service and assess value, impact, and risk using different measures than IT departments and differentiates library and IT perspectives on an "end user." This difference can have a cascading effect on library IT and can be a cause of discord between library-centric and organization-wide IT departments. Although the move to cloud or virtualized platforms may be seen as a way to bridge these differences, it can also lead to more complicated and interdependent relationships.

One way of bridging this gap is for libraries to select service assessment models that share common ground with IT departments while also leaving room for these differences. Despite the fact that they may start with an IT-centric world view, IT service models are useful in this area because they include ways to differentiate internal and external customers and include considerations for capacity and risk while keeping a focus on user service expectations. One model that provides a common vocabulary for these discussions is Addy's "Components of a Service" model (2007, 51), which uses concentric circles to show the relationship among the concepts of capacity, control, and metrics derived from a single-level relationship (e.g., IT to organizational unit support). Addy's model places user requirements at the center and surrounds them with issues including service capacity, service-level requirements, contractual obligations, costs, security, metrics, methods for delivery, and methods for service administration. Although this model is successful at outlining the relationships between IT management, systems, and end users, it does not show how to balance the security, access, and service-level needs of multiple sets of end users or multiple tiers of IT administrators (e.g., infrastructure, platform, application, and service). A library-centric IT service model commonly needs to differentiate IT management, library administration, librarian, and patron uses of a system. Likewise, it is common for libraries to require some form of multidepartmental administrative arrangement in which the library may handle application and perhaps platform administration but not operating system administration.

Table 3.1 groups some of the main themes discussed in chapter 2 using the TOE model and elaborates the roles of administration, service deployment, and organization-specific issues such as staffing, financial considerations, and legal factors. Each of these areas can be considered within the context of organizational IT, library IT, and patron-focused end users. The exploration of these factors delves into complex issues of measures of cost and success, organizational values, and preferences that are not easily quantified. In addition, calculating broader costs (e.g., total IT service cost as opposed to IT hardware and software costs) and return on investment (ROI) can be difficult given the mix of staffing expenses and IT acquisition costs, differences in software licensing and subscription costs, and

TABLE 3.1
Factors Influencing IT Service Adoption

Focus	Issues
Technical	access levels, administration, capacity planning, deliverables, replication, scaling, security
Organizational	access (who has), accountability, coaccess, cost sharing, disaster planning, responsibility boundaries
Staffing	administrative operations, capacity, collaboration, development support, expertise, operational support, workflow integration
Financial	capital planning, cost, efficiency, return on investment
Legal	contracts, data ownership, nondisclosure agreements, privacy, SLAs, terms of service
Environmental	preferred system, functional requirements, external regulations, external obligations, interorganizational agreements

impact of term-of-service life cycle. Measuring the quality and impact of these services can be more difficult than measuring cost or ROI, but they may be better measures of an organization's view of the value of an information service and can be helpful in guiding decision making for IT platform adoption. Measures that can be useful in quantifying service value include desired service uptime as compared to real-world availability, the opportunity cost of service downtime, absolute or relative service utilization measures (e.g., through log file analysis or Google Analytics), and an analysis of system relationships and dependencies.

Several issues in table 3.1—such as access levels, administration, accountability, responsibility boundaries, coadministration, and coaccess—likely require complex agreements in cases where the library seeks to share administrative roles with an organizational or external IT department. In addition, negotiating SLAs that are tuned toward assuring a level of support focused on end-user or public operations (e.g., evening and weekend support for research tools) as opposed to staff-focused or business operations (e.g., Monday–Friday business hours) can be key to high-quality service deployment. Finally, it is worth noting that the factors listed in table 3.1 also need to be considered within the context of the service or service component being analyzed. All IT services include infrastructure (e.g., computing hardware, operating systems, networking, power, and cooling), platform (e.g., operating system, software stacks, development, and deployment frameworks), application (e.g., an information system that fills a single or multiple roles), and service elements (e.g., an end-point resource that provides some form of information service based on the functions of the application). Depending on the type of IT system being examined, one or more of these areas will need to be considered from the perspectives discussed in table 3.1. This can make comparing a traditional nonvirtualized environment (in which each of the four technology levels may be administered by the library) with an outsourced or SaaS application difficult. The following sections explore some of these factors in more detail and can serve as a starting point for libraries considering IT alternatives.

TECHNICAL FACTORS

Of all issues to consider when exploring cloud-based and virtualized services, technical issues are likely to take center stage. Understanding the technical work required when a library takes on virtualized and cloud computing is an important first step that can help guide decisions about capacity and long-term sustainability.

Infrastructure Administration

The administration of infrastructure-level services focuses on core elements including network, server, and operating systems. Infrastructure-level administration often comes with beginning-to-end responsibility for an information service and requires the ability to design and deploy a hardware (both virtualized or physical) infrastructure, install and configure software, secure and maintain distinct IT components (e.g., server, network, security), and manage change in service configuration and deployment. This requires a familiarity with security measures (e.g., firewalls, user access, and system updates) and IT service management (e.g., service configuration, deployment, backup, failover, and depreciation) and a granular understanding of the implications of system design on the information service. In a cloud environment this also means a wider familiarity with cloud service elements that constitute an IaaS environment (e.g., server images, volume snapshots, security groups). The NIST reference model expands on infrastructure-level skill requirements with ten technical factors to be considered in relation to cloud computing adoption (Fang et al. 2011):

1. Creating, accessing, updating, and deleting data objects in clouds
2. Moving virtual machines and virtual appliances between clouds
3. Selecting the best IaaS vendor for a private externally hosted cloud
4. Tools for monitoring and managing multiple clouds
5. Migrating data between clouds
6. Single sign-on access to multiple clouds
7. Orchestrated processes across clouds
8. Discovering cloud resources
9. Evaluating SLAs and penalties
10. Auditing clouds

Some of these tasks are highly technical and require infrastructure-level expertise. For example, creating, managing, and migrating virtual machines requires understanding how to allocate infrastructure resources and configure systems and applications. Other tasks including evaluating SLAs, discovering new cloud resources, and auditing cloud services are important for all approaches to cloud computing. Given the complexity inherent in many of these technical factors, it may be necessary to choose those that are more important in a particular environment. For example, whereas patron privacy and quality of service are major issues in libraries, single sign-on or fully interoperable cloud environments may not be necessary when selecting cloud-based information services.

Libraries can find it challenging to locate the resources in-house to manage technology infrastructure but also may find that cloud providers are reducing the complexity of these systems and lowering the costs (both financial and operational) to implement and manage these services. Though this list of required skills may be daunting, the ability to manage infrastructure-level services can be helpful for libraries given their tendency to adopt information services from different vendors or open-source communities. For librarians seeking to develop expertise in infrastructure administration, becoming familiar with local virtualization platforms such as Oracle's VirtualBox (http://virtualbox.org) and with cloud virtualization platforms offered by IaaS providers (e.g., Amazon, Rackspace, or Microsoft) is a good first step. These skills transfer easily, since the conceptual understanding required to use Amazon's platform is mirrored in other providers (e.g., the understanding of CPU time–based charging, storage resources, firewall resources, monitoring services, authentication services). Although specific services depend on the platform or application deployed, having an understanding of infrastructure-level capacity helps when librarians or IT administrators are faced with the process of designing a cloud-based or virtualized system.

Platform Administration

Technical aspects of platform support typically include an emphasis on the software components that constitute an end-user-facing application. For example, a content management system running on WordPress requires familiarity with Apache, MySQL, PHP, and WordPress plug-ins and may require familiarity with authentication systems (e.g., LDAP, Shibboleth) and secure web connections (e.g., SSL). Depending on the platform selected, other skills may be required including programming familiarity, an understanding of web service architecture, or a more granular understanding of server infrastructure.

In a PaaS cloud environment, platform administration may require familiarity with a specific suite or configuration of web services. For example, Google Apps Engine (http://code.google.com/appengine/) requires users to design their applications within a specific framework that includes a database platform, programming framework, and web-service deployment architecture. Because libraries often have limited IT resources, they may find platform and application administration to be more approachable than infrastructure administration. On a limited scale this enables libraries to deploy and manage applications that they might not otherwise be able to support. On a larger scale, however, this can lead to a complex and unsustainable IT management infrastructure. Chapter 4 explores PaaS examples in depth, considers PaaS environments that enable simple operation at larger scales, and discusses these advantages and concerns.

Application Administration

Libraries may choose to avoid infrastructure and platform administration, but they often want to administer the application itself. Internally administered applications can lead to more adaptive and rapidly deployed services and give libraries a sense of control over their IT environment. At the same time, application administration requires an understanding of application functions and, depending on the service, may require an understanding of the underlying technical infrastructure, including the role of computational, storage, and network resources. Technical knowledge specific to application administration includes familiarity with data models, configuration options, and end-user service elements and the ability to implement processes that leverage application tools (e.g., bulk-processing tools, user authentication connectors). As with infrastructure- and platform-level work, this may require familiarity with programming languages; related organizational IT services and common data processing; and workflow, authentication, and automation processes.

Where staff resources or the capacity for application administration is not available, libraries may choose to focus on SaaS solutions that include an advanced level of application administration as part of the service. Examples of this service in the library world include SerialsSolutions Summon service (www.serialssolutions.com/discovery/summon/) and OCLC's Worldshare Management Service (www.oclc.org/webscale/), both of which offload the bulk of IT and application administration work from libraries and provide advanced administrative functions through browser-based interfaces. In contrast, where there is a high level of application administration expertise in-house, libraries may seek IaaS or PaaS solutions that offload server administration but provide a level of access to the server that enables customization. As with infrastructure and platform administration elements, matching staff expertise to the level of customization desired for an application is important to ensure sustainable and secure management of library information services. The shift to web-based technologies, including cascading style sheets, HTML, and JavaScript for common library applications such as content management systems, means that libraries may be able to hold onto the ability to customize user interfaces and application functionality while also relying on SaaS solutions for applications. This is not always possible, however; many providers promise the ability to customize the end-user experience, but it is important for libraries to ask specific questions in relation to the interface modifications they are seeking.

Security

There are a host of security issues that affect both the comfort level for adoption of cloud services and also the sustainability of a cloud-based service once it is selected. In general, the goal of system security is to prevent unauthorized access to IT infrastructure, administrative services, and user-facing services. It also includes preventing interruptions in connectivity and the hardening of systems against intrusion attempts using open ports, cracked passwords, software vulnerabilities, and back-door and man-in-the middle attacks. The work in this area includes a necessary focus on traditional IT security measures including active monitoring, firewall and application control, penetration testing, and incident management and response, but it also involves new security issues related specifically to cloud platforms, such as virtual private networking, multiplatform monitoring, data center certification, and trusted user authentication (Constantin 2011). For librarians interested in learning more about security management, Limoncelli et al.'s (2001) guide to system administration provides a foundation for approaching IT security issues and includes a focus on the role of policy and auditing in ensuring consistent and durable system security.

A central policy and procedure checklist may help organizations with security monitoring, but other areas in a cloud environment also need attention. For example, the addition of multiple platforms in a cloud computing environment means that security concerns need to be assessed both for individual systems and for the connections between systems. In addition to the common security risk areas of authentication, server isolation, and data protection, cloud-centric risk areas include security holes in the selected hypervisor platform, the risks associated with running in a common virtualized environment, and the risks associated with operating servers in a public or community network (e.g., firewalls, access, file permissions).

At a server, platform, or application level, security approaches include limiting access via password/secure key authentication methods, blocking access by firewall use, using internal encryption to secure data on your servers, and using virtual private networks (VPNs) to create an additional level of security surrounding your IT infrastructure. An internal IT security policy should include acceptable use, monitoring, privacy remote access, network connectivity, and log retention policies (Limoncelli et al. 2001, 124). In addition, organizations that implement externally virtualized or cloud-based services should obtain or define policies that ensure data integrity, preserve local ownership of resources located in the cloud, and ensure the integrity of the overall cloud platform. Although there are risks associated with operating in a public or community cloud environment, cloud virtualization systems have been designed to ensure the isolation of virtual machines. Vendor assurances can help mitigate the perceived risks of public or community cloud platforms and are good building blocks on which to base a local security policy. For example, Amazon has obtained certifications and accreditations that document its ability to provide secure cloud services (http://aws.amazon.com/security/#certifications). Using these certifications as a base level to evaluate infrastructure security can help organizations identify suitable cloud candidates. In addition, a thorough understanding of the details of these security policies can help organizations focus their work on other areas of vulnerability. More details on provider-level security and assurances are discussed in the legal and policy section of this chapter.

One complication that can come with cloud computing platforms is the need to replicate security measures in each adopted platform or vendor. Therefore, having a clear and consistent policy on what measures are in place and how they are implemented (e.g., how user accounts are created, managed, and audited) helps simplify the adoption of new computing environments. This does not necessarily mean the centralization of security responsibilities but rather that the organization as a whole needs to be well informed about the real risks and management practices required in a cloud environment. For example, in SaaS environments it may make sense to delegate these tasks to a mid-level administrative user rather than routing them through an IT department. In contrast, the level of access and expertise required to administer user accounts in an IaaS environment properly likely means that these tasks need to be managed by staff familiar with the processes and associated risks. In both cases, however, creating a layered security policy can help extend access to the appropriate levels while preventing compromises. In the Amazon EC2 environment, for example, security groups are used as a cloud environment–level firewall that allows the grouping of servers in access groups. This level of security is offered in addition to server-level firewall options and could allow a distributed security management policy in which mid-level administrators have a higher level of access to server resources because there is little risk that they can make their systems vulnerable from outside of the organization's virtual server infrastructure.

The NIST cloud computing model emphasizes several important tasks to undertake to ensure proper cloud security. These include elements mentioned above (e.g., managing access, mitigating risk associated with common IT use through firewalls, and detecting intrusion) in addition to designing applications that leverage cloud features to enhance, rather than undermine, security. There are also client elements such as web browser security and the use of client/server security certificates which, when implemented properly, can ensure a higher level of client/server security (Fang et al. 2011, 39). A final area of key importance, particularly in integrating IaaS and PaaS environments, is the sharing of authentication keys and accounts. RightScale, in particular, relies on the establishment of trusted relationships using administrative accounts and access keys with IaaS cloud platforms. It is worth noting that, once these trust relationships are established, users in the RightScale service have the ability to control at a very granular level the services running in those other environments. Likewise, many of the Amazon application programming interface (API) services rely on preshared keys. If these keys are saved on client machines, direct access to Amazon IaaS elements is available to any user of that machine. Cloud providers are beginning to offer ways to compartmentalize access to resources using identity management tools that allow system administrators to monitor which users access infrastructure-level resources and limit access based on login or key credentials.

Library-Specific IT Support

Determining local capacity for implementing and administering cloud resources is grounded in an understanding of personnel skill and time availability, technical needs, and financial resources. These factors need to be compared with projected service cost and impact to get an understanding of how important a given service or cloud platform is. As our exploration of infrastructure, application, and platform administration shows, technical skill and capacity play a large role in selecting, implementing, and managing a service. Likewise, depending on the cloud service selected, there may be upper limits to the capacity of that given system. As our exploration of IaaS providers in chapter 5 shows, the approach to and costs of implementing a scalable service on these platforms vary widely. For example Netflix viewed the latency in the Amazon EBS platform as a capacity-limiting factor and so redesigned its web services to utilize Amazon S3 (Cockroft et al. 2011). Although example emphasizes the ability of IaaS providers to scale in response to demand, it sidesteps the limitations to local expertise, physical infrastructure, or disaster management that can make leveraging these features difficult. Because of this, it is important to be familiar with the elements of IT service management, security, and local capacity so that local and cloud-based capacity can be determined and an appropriate system selected.

One reason often cited for libraries moving to cloud systems is the need for greater IT support than is available locally. In some cases the need focuses on specific platforms, and in others the need focuses on data issues or scalability requirements that are not available in a local IT shop. In choosing to migrate to cloud solutions, however, libraries need to be aware of the IT services that must be provided by local IT. Some examples of service support required by libraries include network infrastructure and Internet access, domain name service (DNS) resolution, organizational authentication, organizational user or patron data, and firewall or VPN service.

In particular, having the ability to work with organizational IT to define new DNS entries for external servers, to open firewall rules to allow easier communication between internal and cloud-based servers, and to employ VPN as a means to limit access to the servers are three key services that facilitate the migration to cloud platforms. These services both form a trusted relationship between organizational IT and the library and demonstrate the limit of support requested by library IT. An SLA that explicitly outlines the types of services supported and the limits of responsibility can go a long way toward redefining the relationship of the library to the organization's IT department and addressing concerns that can initially seem insurmountable.

ORGANIZATIONAL FACTORS

Although local IT resources or technical expertise may drive which cloud solutions a library considers, organizational factors including risk tolerance, finance and budgeting environment, available staff resources, and fit of cloud solutions with overall service goals may be equally important. Increasingly, libraries are able to find cloud solutions (particularly SaaS) that fit their specialized needs and organizational culture. These include not only SaaS-based vendor services but also cloud environments dedicated to higher education institutions (e.g., Eduserve, www.eduserv.org.uk) and to government agencies including Amazon (http://aws.amazon.com/federal/), Microsoft Azure (www.microsoft.com/industry/government), GovDelivery (http://govdelivery.com), and government-coordinated clearinghouses such as apps.gov (http://apps.gov). These cloud providers are examples of community clouds that provide value-added service by addressing legal and operational requirements specific to particular communities. Amazon's government cloud environment, for example, includes additional regulatory assurances and physical separation from other cloud environments at the server and network levels.

Budgeting and Service Subscription

Libraries turning to library-specific virtualization and cloud solutions often find that the budgeting and subscription terms provided by the vendor recognize the approaches typical of that industry, but they may also find that cloud providers from other areas are not used to working with libraries and other nonprofit institutions. In many of the cloud services explored in chapters 4 and 5, subscription terms are measured in hours or months rather than annually based. This can make budgeting and cost prediction more difficult and challenging. In addition, many cloud providers including Amazon and Microsoft rely primarily on credit cards as a form of payment and do not support purchase orders or other long-term subscription models by default.

Several PaaS and SaaS solutions are specifically for libraries. These include for-profit companies such as SerialsSolutions (http://serialssolutions.com), LibLime (http://liblime.com), Equinox (http://esilibrary.com), and ByWater Solutions (http://bywatersolutions.com/) as well as nonprofit organizations such as Lyrasis (http://lyrasis.org), OCLC (http://oclc.org), DuraCloud (http://duracloud.org), and Omeka (http://omeka.net). These nonprofit organizations (with the exception of OCLC) support the implementation of open-source platforms (e.g., DSpace and Omeka) that might not otherwise be implementable by libraries. For libraries interested in non-library-specific application hosting, there are companies such as LisHost (http://lishost.org) that focus on providing more generalized web hosting services for libraries. Selecting one of these cloud providers sidesteps some of the budgeting and payment issues libraries are likely to encounter with other cloud providers but also limits the platforms available for cloud adoption. Whether this is an issue depends entirely on organizational factors and preferred services.

Disaster and Recovery Planning

In a traditional IT environment, disaster planning involves creating system backups, creating a service restoration plan, managing an IT infrastructure to enable redundancy and availability, and colocating backups and valuable data in multiple locations. Cloud computing and virtualized solutions enable new approaches to durable and disaster-proof service but also pose new requirements in the implementation of these services, including replication across cloud regions, recovery plans that include multiple cloud providers, and backups on cloud-based storage systems. Reese (2009, 119) discusses a range of issues related to disaster recovery in the cloud including data backups, server configuration storage, server redundancy, and disaster monitoring. Velte et al. (2009, 37) mention several benefits of using the cloud for backup including reduced data loss, simplified monitoring, faster recovery, and improved security.

Whatever the benefits, a cloud-based backup, replication, and recovery strategy needs to be considered within the context of organizational risk tolerance and legal liability. For example, when organizations shift away from local IT infrastructure to cloud platforms there is an increased need to support service replication across multiple cloud providers, backup data on multiple cloud networks, and automate processes to ensure that the library can leverage the backup, replication, and scalability features typically associated with cloud platforms. Cloud computing is still a relatively new technology and, though rare, cloud providers periodically

Issues to Consider for Service Durability

Regardless of platform or type of service, consider the following issues when adopting a cloud platform:

- Database backup and restoration procedures.
- Replicated storage of long-term digital resources.
- Documentation of server configuration and service interactions. In an optimal situation, this would be implemented using an automatic configuration system (see chapter 5).
- Automatic redundancy of cloud services within a cloud provider. A key method of avoiding downtime is to implement services that feature continuous data protection, automatic scaling, and multizone replication of services.

experience downtime related to software bugs and system configuration anomalies. On February 29, 2012, for example, a leap day software bug in the Microsoft Azure platform caused systemwide downtime for Azure customers for several hours (Babcock 2012). Likewise, in 2011 Amazon had its own issues when a misconfigured network caused widespread problems in its Virginia cloud region (Babcock 2011). These service outages were both fairly short-term and did not result in long-term data loss, but still they underscore the importance of being comfortable with and planning for backup and service replication strategies.

One of the key challenges to a manageable and successful backup and recovery policy for libraries moving to cloud platforms is maintaining consistent approaches across multiple cloud providers. Another complication is ensuring that your library is in compliance with organizational policies. This can be complicated by the fact that many IT organizations have backup procedures geared toward traditional backup methods (e.g., tape-based backups or server-rebuild processes). In a cloud environment, bandwidth limitations and local infrastructure can make backing up to local tape difficult, and the cost of transferring backup data sets across the network can make this approach cost prohibitive. There are cloud-based services that support low-cost, high-durability backups including BackBlaze (http://backblaze.com) and MozyPro (http://mozypro.com), but overall the trend is away from tape backups for cloud-based services. Some traditional backup applications such as Amanda (www.amanda.com) have been updated to leverage the open storage of Amazon S3 using open-source industry-standard backup tools. This may be preferable to system or volume snapshots, which are available only from within the cloud provider's system. In contrast, Amanda uses traditional archiving and compression tools that do not rely on a proprietary system. By backing up to S3, libraries can preserve the ability to download their backups at any time or via an automated process. It is worth noting that there are services that move in the other direction (e.g., using S3 as the redundant backup for local data). For example, using the Amazon Storage Gateway (http://aws.amazon.com/storagegateway/), subscribers can replicate data from local or other cloud-based services in the Amazon S3 system. This provides users the benefit of backing up to a service with a defined SLA and in a redundant and geographically replicated system. In 2012 Amazon also introduced an S3-backed storage solution called Amazon Glacier (http://aws.amazon.com/glacier/) that features built-in data replication and fixity checking services. Glacier is marketed as a tape-backup replacement service and achieves cost reductions by gearing the service around long-term storage assurances rather than immediate retrieval.

In addition to maintaining suitable backups of data, in the cloud environment it is also important to develop a means to back up and restore server configurations. In an optimal situation the backup and replication approach includes the ability to deploy servers and data onto different cloud providers. Although this is likely to be an issue only for libraries adopting PaaS and IaaS solutions, it is important for libraries looking toward SaaS solutions to determine whether service providers have a plan for managing backup, recovery, and replication of services. There is an emerging set of businesses focused on service replication across cloud providers that fall into the NIST category of cloud broker. One example is RightScale (http://rightscale.com). This service supports multiple IaaS providers and synchronizes data and services back to a local private cloud environment or to other public clouds.

Regardless of the type of cloud or virtualized solution selected, replication and backup are key issues. Some important considerations in these decisions: (1) How important is a secondary cloud or localized service backup? (2) Which service works best with local capacity? (3) How important are short-, mid-, and long-term backups? (4) Is continuous data protection more important than durable long-term backups? (5) How important are industry standard backup platforms as compared to proprietary systems?

This fifth consideration can be a major stumbling block for libraries seeking to store data in the cloud. For example, libraries that are using the cloud as their primary digital object and metadata storage platform need to identify a solution that relies on traditional storage, version control, and bit-checking methods. In contrast, cloud and virtualization platforms make it much easier to take snapshots of file systems and save space by recording only the difference between versions of a file system. This process is highly efficient both for taking backups and restoring them, but it creates issues for organizations that want to have access to archived data using traditional file system tools (e.g., mountable file system and compression tools).

Service-Level Agreements and Terms of Service

SLAs and terms of service are important documents that define the relationship between cloud computing providers and subscribers. SLAs define the level of service assured with a cloud service, including elements such as system uptime, system security, support contacts, and response-time agreements. Libraries may be familiar with SLA elements given their experience negotiating with electronic resource vendors. In contrast, terms of service focus on higher-level issues such as liability, legal recourse, and the general use of the service by subscribers. Terms of service and SLAs serve different purposes but in general address how a service can be used and what behaviors are acceptable for both providers and subscribers. Limoncelli et al. (2001) list several considerations in negotiating SLAs, including response times in various service situations, nonperformance issues, performance assessment, guaranteed system performance, and service uptime/backup routines. Trappler (2010) expands this list to include infrastructure capacity, security, and error correction time.

With so many measures it can be difficult to understand which are essential and what the real meaning of uptime assurances is. As a good example, Conry-Murray (2009) documented uptime guarantees by different cloud providers in a 2009 report and found them ranging from 99.7 percent to 100 percent depending on provider. Though 99.7 percent might seem good enough, it leaves room for over two hours of downtime per month. Reese (2009, 55) rightly observes that even a short period of downtime may have major implications for information services. In addition, because cloud services are often based on multiple service providers, measuring service quality can be very uncertain. This difference in perspective became apparent when Amazon experienced service downtime in one zone early in 2011 and caused downtime for services that had not been designed to operate in multiple availability zones (Leong 2011). In fact, Amazon's availability definition is only for services that operate in multiple availability zones, meaning that organizations are not fully supported unless they configure their cloud services in the specified manner.

An additional challenge with SLAs is the difficulty of working with multiple vendors and agreements while trying to implement a sustainable and consistent service architecture. Making this process more difficult is the fact that libraries can find it difficult, if not impossible, to negotiate the SLA with large cloud providers. IaaS providers in particular provide an SLA for a broad system infrastructure and are not in the business of providing tailored support. Although not always realistic, there are ways around this one-size-fits-all approach. First, government organizations are gaining access to specialized IaaS environments that operate under specialized terms through Amazon and other IaaS providers. It may pay to find a community cloud provider that recognizes issues unique to your institution. Additionally, educational organizations can often negotiate with corporations for enterprise-wide solutions or can choose to (in the case of Amazon) pay for a higher level of service support. Finally, paying attention to built-in support levels and the availability of customer service can help libraries find the right fit in an IaaS provider. These providers all offer similar services, but their approaches to customer service vary considerably.

Terms of service, SLAs, and other use agreements between subscriber and cloud provider can be daunting to say the least. These agreements spell out areas of legal liability, recourse, indemnification, and other issues that may seem excessive for

Interpreting Contracts

Interpreting a cloud computing contract may involve a new area of expertise for IT staff. As always, consulting legal counsel, collections management, or administrative staff can be helpful. Some key areas to focus on in SLAs and terms of service include these:

- Duration of contract and termination procedures: What constitutes subscription and termination? How are renewals handled?
- Payment methods: What payment methods are supported, and what payment terms are extended? What is the procedure for termination if payment lapses?
- Legal jurisdiction: What jurisdiction and laws apply to the contract, and what limits are placed on issues of arbitration and liability?
- Indemnification, warranty, and service assurance: What warranties does the provider agree to and how do these assurances relate to the SLA? What liabilities does the provider recognize?
- Privacy policy: Under what conditions are customer data made available to external organizations?
- Data ownership and retention upon service discontinuation: Who owns data located on the cloud service, and what happens to that data when the service agreement is discontinued?
- Service integrity: What does the provider define as a complete service, and how does it assure that its service remains operational?
- Data disclosure and service monitoring: Does the provider regularly disclose data regarding customers? Does it monitor traffic, stored data, or processes?
- Data and service location: Where are the data housed by the cloud provider physically located? What implications does this have for your organization's adherence to organizational policy and legal regulations?

A thorough exploration of these topics would easily fill a chapter, but good resources include policy papers by Jaeger et al. (2008, 2009) and Bradshaw et al. (2010).

low-level cloud adoption. There are several issues to consider, though, and libraries are best served by following up with legal counsel if the reading and interpretation of agreements pose problems for adoption.

Service Capacity

Libraries are unique adopters of cloud computing in that their main focus is on providing information services rather than on managing information technology. Libraries also tend to adopt multiple platforms to fill the needs of their patrons and may encounter challenges when attempting to gain support for these systems within their organizations. Though virtualized and cloud solutions can help with this situation, they can also create an environment in which library IT service is fragmented onto multiple providers and platforms.

IT service organizations familiar with service management approaches such as ITIL or ITSM may have ways of measuring the impact of a selected information system on an organization's IT support capacity. Common measures include available IT infrastructure, IT staff support availability, and application administration capacity. These departments may view virtualization and cloud computing as a way to improve local capacity from the perspective of either infrastructure or IT staff time. As a library or IT department turns toward cloud or virtualized solutions that involve direct system or application management, it is important that it take a systematic approach that leverages literature on IT service management. For example, before implementing multiple IaaS or PaaS solutions, libraries should also design a service management and replication plan that accounts for staff resources, IT resources, and ongoing expenses. A core part of this consideration is workflow integration and operational overlap. In regards to service capacity, it is important to consider challenges to sharing data, compatibility issues in workflow integration, and loss of efficiency that may come when working with multiple virtualized or cloud solutions. For example, data access over an Internet-based network connection is likely to see more latency than when accessed over an internal network connection. This may not be problematic for short bursts of data, but it can be challenging when interacting with large amounts of data or when streaming audio or video materials over a cloud connection. To work around the latency issue in particular, cloud providers may offer dedicated network connections for upload/download, may allow the subscriber to ship large datasets on physical storage media to a data-loading department, and may feature high-speed internal networks to facilitate transfer of data inside the provider's cloud network.

Likewise, if libraries turn to cloud solutions, it is important that they carefully consider the implications related to system interoperability. Because many library administrative services are being offered via browser-based web services, traditional efficiency techniques such as client macros, application switching, and keyboard shortcuts may not be usable for connecting disparate applications.

ENVIRONMENTAL FACTORS

Infrastructure, Platform, and Service Costs

The ease with which costs can be projected varies with cloud platform, but estimates often involve more than accounting for direct run-time and licensing costs. Determining direct costs for SaaS solutions and entirely local virtualized or nonvirtualized solutions may prove to be easier to calculate than for public or community PaaS and IaaS solutions, if only because the purchasing approach for private IT service and SaaS service follows capital investment or yearly subscription models. In contrast, nonprivate PaaS and IaaS solutions are often charged at per-hour or per-bit levels, and estimating the costs for each of the elements (e.g., CPU time, network traffic, storage, backups, reserved IP addresses) can affect the reliability of these projections.

Considerations for Calculating Cost

Financial factors relevant to moving to cloud environments include a need to support ongoing instead of capital costs, an ability to pay for cloud services using the payment terms available from a given cloud provider, and the ability to plan for and support long-term costs associated with cloud computing (e.g., long-term preservation of digital resources and migration costs). The ability to pay for cloud services using a supported payment method, as it turns out, can be significant for some organizations. As of this writing, Amazon EC2 services are available only via credit card transactions, except for large subscribers. This can create problems in small organizations where a payment method might be tied to a specific individual's corporate card; it can be a deal breaker in organizations where credit card transactions are not supported at all. In these cases, alternate cloud brokers can be selected that support a common payment method.

A second key financial consideration is whether a library's current software licenses and platforms support migration to the cloud. Software licensing is important in both server operating system and higher-level applications. In some cases new licenses are required for cloud computing, particularly in the case of proprietary or managed operating systems (http://aws.amazon.com/windows/; http://aws.amazon.com/rhel/). In other cases, specific services are licensed in an SaaS model (http://salesforce.com). In extreme cases, it may not be possible to implement software in a cloud environment when licensing terms are strictly tied to traditional IT paradigms (e.g., per-CPU, per-user, or license-server models). Although higher-level library application licensing may not be affected by an implementation in cloud computing environments, it is important to check, particularly when a scaling infrastructure is likely to be chosen that would create additional run-time copies of the software.

It is worth noting that, although the shift to cloud computing has posed problems for open-source adoption in libraries, open-source software also simplifies the implementation of IT on cloud platforms given the lack of licensing issues. It is entirely possible to create a cloud infrastructure based wholly on open-source platforms, including operating systems, web publishing systems, and a range of library-specific applications. It is possible to use only open-source solutions in IaaS and PaaS environments, less likely to do so with SaaS solutions. Further, when libraries turn to open sources for operating system and core infrastructure elements (e.g., system backups and web servers), they may also take on additional system management responsibilities. One of the main areas of importance in this situation is the necessity to select open-source components that feature regular security and functional updates. Amazon seeks to make this process more sustainable by offering a certified version of Linux in its server templates (http://aws.amazon.com/amazon-linux-ami/). Other communities such as Ubuntu and CentOS offer regular updates as well. In addition, open-source platforms such as RedHat (http://redhat.com) offer paid support levels for Linux-based operating systems.

Determine Actual Cost and ROI

The two ROI models explored in this section come from Reese's (2009) work on cloud adoption and Feldman's (2012) exploration of the use of ROI by cloud subscribers. Reese (2009, 50) uses an ROI worksheet that includes categories for up-front, labor, recurring, capital, licensing, and subscription costs associated with both traditional and cloud-based IT. His recommendation is to estimate costs over a three-year period as a way to enable comparison to traditional IT services.

Reese's approach focuses on itemizing hardware costs and grouping labor costs into a single sum and includes an estimation of the cost of performance loss that may be a factor in selecting capacity in the cloud (e.g., an organization may select a mid-capacity cloud server that just meets current demand rather than overbuying capacity for a physical server). This cost of performance loss can be mitigated by designing scalable systems and actually could be viewed from the other direction (e.g., the capital cost of unutilized capacity).

In contrast, Feldman's (2012, 19) ROI approach uses capital costs, operational costs, future capital cost (or savings), staffing impact, time savings for non-IT staff, resource provisioning (e.g., hardware acquisition/setup time), network expenses, implementation cost, and utility costs as factors. Whereas Reese's calculations describe a wholly local or wholly cloud-based infrastructure in which capital investment savings realized from cloud deployment result in an overall lower total cost for cloud services, Feldman's ROI analysis suggests that the most economical approach focuses on using private cloud services that support public cloud bursting (e.g., Eucalyptus, OpenStack, or Cloudstack) and differentiates long-term investments from short-term capacity need.

These conclusions show how difficult calculating ROI can be for cloud services and introduce three distinct approaches: nonvirtualized, private/public cloud, fully public/community cloud. It is worth noting that in making this claim Feldman is pointing to large-scale companies such as DreamWorks and Zynga, both of which

Cloud Bursting

Cloud bursting is the ability to scale computing and storage resources quickly from a private cloud into a public or community cloud environment using the same tools and standards employed in the private cloud. Two providers in particular, Amazon and RackSpace, support cloud bursting using different private cloud platforms. In March 2012, Amazon announced a formal agreement with Eucalyptus to design its cloud system using the same application programming interface tool design that was first deployed by Amazon (Eucalyptus 2012). Likewise, RackSpace was key in the development and release of OpenStack and is building toward the ability to migrate private OpenStack deployments easily to RackSpace services (Moorman 2011). In addition, data centers such as Internap (http://internap.com) are beginning to offer private cloud platforms using the OpenStack platform, enabling a new type of externally sourced private and public cloud architecture.

have "burst level" capacity needs that far exceed the ongoing resource needs of most libraries for several years (e.g., 10 million CPU hours) (Feldman 2012, 6). This means that many libraries could find that their calculations more closely match Reese's view, in which an organization saves resources by making a focused investment in just a single type of computing platform. Figure 3.1 includes a combination of these potential costs in a single ROI matrix.

Figure 3.1 groups cost areas into four sections: initial, ongoing, service management, and labor. The specifics of each area depend on an institution's resources but could include firewalls, load balancing, network switches, Internet traffic expenses, and hardware servers. Such a model is useful as a checklist, but it can lead to a complicated cost calculation in organizations like libraries that often operate as a subunit within a larger organization. For example, libraries are often dealing with a set level of IT infrastructure that is either nonreplaceable or has no direct costs (e.g., an organizational firewall) but may see direct costs based on server acquisition need. Expanding out the cost of an IT service in both a physical environment and cloud-based environment can be difficult in this context but

Cost		Internal non-virtualized	Private cloud	External PaaS/IaaS	External SaaS
Up-front resources	Networking				
	Servers				
	Storage				
	Software licensing				
Ongoing resources	Networking				
	Servers				
	Storage				
	Software licensing				
Support services	Service monitoring				
	Service auditing				
	Service provisioning				
Labor	IT labor				
	Non-IT labor				

FIGURE 3.1
Generalized cost calculation template

may provide some assistance in breaking down different costs associated with cloud-based options.

Another factor that complicates cloud cost calculation is the expected duration of the service being implemented. Reese recommends projecting costs over a three-year period; Feldman differentiates "start-up" and "enterprise" adoptions and argues that as organizations move to an enterprise level they are likely to find more cost savings in running a private cloud environment with public cloud bursting capacity. Rather than think in terms of start-up versus enterprise, libraries may want to consider the projected longevity of an information service instead. This can help an organization understand the potential cost savings from up-front capital investments versus ongoing cloud investments in short- and long-term services. It also can make the calculation of ROI more complex. This likely involves choosing or adhering to a depreciation schedule and having a detailed understanding of the technology costs that will and will not go away in a cloud service. To help with these calculations, Reese provides formulas to calculate cost over the life of the service and to determine current technology value (2009, 53, 12). Cloud providers, particularly IaaS providers, may provide cost calculators—for example, Amazon (http://calculator.s3.amazonaws.com/calc5.html), Microsoft Azure (www.microsoft.com/windowsazure/pricing-calculator/), and RightScale (www.rightscale.com/tco-calculator/).

Another important factor in cost calculation, particularly for libraries, is data storage and data transfer costs. A common method for planning for backup costs over time is to estimate the amount of change in data expected over a month and multiply total storage by that percentage (e.g., if you expect a 15 percent change in a month, your backup charges are 1.15 times storage costs). The fact that backed-up data are entirely replicated on cloud services can make storage costs seem very expensive, but many cloud services including Amazon's S3 and Glacier services include automatic replication and redundancy as part of the storage service. This does not eliminate the need for backups, but for organizations comfortable with this approach to storage the use of version control and unique backups with limited archiving history can lower the overall costs of storage.

Legal and Policy Issues

When libraries are adopting a cloud service, there are policies that need to be considered both within the provider/subscriber relationship and between the subscribers and outside organizations. These relationships are often discussed as terms of service, acceptable use policies, and privacy policies. There are often multiple versions of these policies, particularly for free and paid versions of cloud services. Libraries interested in using free cloud services may find that the default terms of the service pose significant barriers in relation to FERPA, HIIPA, or USA PATRIOT Act regulations. In paid cloud services there are opportunities to negotiate these terms, and libraries can minimize risk by adopting cloud platforms that avoid thorny privacy policy terms or by blocking provider access to subscriber data.

Navigating this range of terms, policies, and agreements can be difficult, if only because of the number of ways agreements can be published or made available. In fact, organizations do not always publish distinct documents and may include privacy policy issues in terms of service document and vice versa (Bradshaw et al. 2010). Outside of the terms of service and acceptable use policies, libraries face legal and policy issues when examining cloud-based or virtualized IT solutions. Although these issues are not largely different from those encountered in a traditional IT environment, cloud computing brings the complications of working with an external vendor. A survey of new IT solutions should include examining government regulations (e.g., HIPPA, FERPA, Patriot Act), software and service licensing issues, and IT standards compliance (Reese 2009, 63). In addition, Gartner's Hype Cycle report (Smith 2010) focuses on privacy issues including personal data and the implications of hardware ownership in public clouds. Jaeger et al. (2009) add data confidentiality and privacy, liability, intellectual property, ownership of data, and auditability as concerns. Trappler (2010) mentions other legal and policy issues including the disposal of data, handling of security breaches, geographic or political location of data, and compliance with legal or governmental requests for data.

These issues are international in scope and complicated by the fact that cloud computing environments can span multiple jurisdictions. Resse (2009, 104) explores three broad factors that should be considered for a given regulation: "How" (e.g., how does an application need to operate to comply with a standard), "Where" (e.g., where can data be stored), and "What" (e.g., what specific elements need to be included in an infrastructure). This approach can help libraries dissect an agreement and better understand the implications.

Cloud computing is also creating difficulties for organizations seeking to use tools that may be located in other countries. In particular, European laws protecting data privacy (Europa 2011) and regulations on data protection and retention (Europa 2010) have specific requirements regarding user consent for data storage and provisions regarding the disposal of unneeded personal data. These regulations pose challenges for vendors seeking to move cloud operations into Europe (O'Brien 2010). In the United States, key federal regulations include HIPPA, FERPA, Patriot Act, Gramm-Leach-Bliley Act, Stored Communications Act, and Sarbanes-Oxley (Jaeger et al. 2008, 2009; Reese 2009). These regulations need to be reviewed to make sure that the migration to the cloud does not compromise organizational adherence to relevant policies.

Although most cloud solutions libraries are likely to work with feature adequate security and privacy assurances, some policies such as the Patriot Act and National Security Letters leave library data vulnerable, given the ability for law enforcement to seize data without notifying the person whose data are requested (Gorham-Oscilowski and Jaeger 2008). This complex legal environment means that libraries must be aware of the risks they assume when moving resources to the cloud. Some suggested approaches include using encryption before sending data to cloud providers, ensuring limited data retention policies, and using system configuration options to prevent retention of private data. In addition, these legal issues have implications for local policy and practice for libraries adopting cloud solutions. For example, data retention is not only an issue for patron circulation data or log data but also applies to stored backups and archives. For libraries that will be responsible for managing their backups in the cloud, there is a real need to be aware of the legal obligation to provide archived data if required.

There are a variety of ways of addressing locally important legal and privacy concerns. First, if an organization seeks absolute privacy, adoption of a private cloud environment is an option that ensures continued local control over services while benefiting from cloud computing. Second, there are community cloud services such as Amazon's GovCloud that offer specialized services for a specific community. In addition, some providers support private cloud options in a public or community cloud. For example, Amazon offers a Virtual Private Cloud environment (http://aws.amazon.com/vpc/) that gives customers the ability to implement cloud infrastructure in a virtual environment that they define. In addition to this virtual isolation, Amazon also supports physical isolation for an additional hourly reservation fee (http://aws.amazon.com/dedicated-instances/).

Despite the procedural and legal concerns raised here, there are ways to handle the risk associated with putting private or sensitive data in the cloud. First, libraries need to implement cloud solutions in a way that guarantees that redundancy and replication are easy to implement and administer. Second, libraries need to have policies that govern loss of access to data and legal issues that may arise from being in the cloud. Finally, although I group legal, policy, and licensing issues under environmental considerations, libraries are likely to find themselves working with organizational standards and organizational data compliance requirements as well. These policies may require data management or nondisclosure agreements to be signed with external providers prior to the sharing of sensitive data such as patron lists or financial account information. The best way to be prepared for such agreements is to engage the management and IT entities in your organization that are responsible for defining and enforcing these policies early on.

PLANNING FOR IMPLEMENTATION

It can be easy to get swept up in the potential cost and efficiency savings outcomes with cloud computing, particularly when focusing on a new service or the opportunity to solve a long-standing problem. For organizations with little existing technical or staffing capacity and no overriding legal or complicating organizational factors, the decision to move to the cloud may be easy. But this situation is likely not the norm, and the choice to move to cloud solutions can be difficult and time consuming. At the same time, libraries are approaching IT issues with a need for highly customized solutions and a need to minimize IT costs while delivering high-quality IT services. For small and medium-sized libraries these choices may frequently focus on SaaS, simple PaaS, or DaaS (a data subscription service supporting a key information system) solutions but may also require advanced PaaS or IaaS solutions for heavily customized or niche services.

For libraries that want to develop expertise in managing IT resources, there are a variety of options. Hosting companies offer platform-specific tutorials focused on launching and managing services (http://aws.amazon.com/articles; http://support.rightscale.com; www.microsoft.com/windowsazure/learn/tutorials/). In addition to platform-specific skills, a general understanding of IT support models helps provide a framework for designing and managing services. Limoncelli et al. (2001) provide a good overview of IT support methods, as does IT Service Management resources (www.itsm.info/). For librarians seeking to understand the elements required to install and configure specific library information systems, there are specialized resources for open-source platforms including DSpace (www.dspace.org/quick-start-guide), Vufind (http://vufind.org/wiki/), Fedora (http://fedora-commons.org), Evergreen (http://open-ils.org), and Koha (http://koha.org).

An important element of cloud computing design and adoption is a full understanding of the additional IT architecture elements required in a cloud environment. Unfortunately, libraries that choose to take on their own IT service management responsibilities run the risk of failing to capitalize on the benefits of cloud computing. Regardless of the solution adopted, it is important to understand the service assurances a provider makes, the requirements a platform must meet to be protected under those assurances, the backup and service restoration options available, and the required administrative activities (e.g., infrastructure, platform, application). For example, because cloud computing often uses commodity hardware, extra attention should be paid to system architecture to ensure that system migration, failover, and restoration are replicable and sustainable. Likewise, it is important to design cloud services that automate these processes as much as possible. These elements are important; still, it is worth keeping in mind the adage "The perfect is the enemy of the good."

Although the process of adopting cloud computing or virtualized solutions is largely similar to the selection and implementation of any IT service, evaluating cloud-based alternatives and fitting the selected service into the wider library IT infrastructure are important steps that tend to add complication. In general, a new cloud platform or service should be evaluated by considering the goal of an information service; available staff, IT, and financial resources to support the service; availability of cloud-based (e.g., SaaS, PaaS, IaaS, DaaS) platforms; and how these alternatives fit with local resources and goals.

The issues explored here can seem overwhelming, but testing a small and minimal-impact service can mitigate the technical complexities, legal/policy risks, and service costs. For those interested in systematic system implementation and management guides, detailed plans are available in Limoncelli et al. (2001), Velte et al. (2009), and Rittinghouse and Ransome (2009).

REFERENCES

Addy, Rob. 2007. *Effective IT Service Management: To ITIL and Beyond!* New York: Springer.

Babcock, Charles. 2011. "Post Mortem: When Amazon's Cloud Turned on Itself." *Information Week*, April 29, 2011. www.informationweek.com/news/cloud-computing/infrastructure/229402534.

———. 2012. "Azure Outage Caused by False Failure Alarms: Microsoft." *Information Week*, March 12, 2012. www.informationweek.com/news/cloud-computing/infrastructure/232602382.

Bradshaw, Simon, Christopher Millard, and Ian Walden. 2010. "Contracts for Clouds: Comparison and Analysis of the Terms and Conditions of Cloud Computing Services." Queen Mary School of Law Legal Studies Research Paper no. 63. http://papers.ssrn.com/sol3/papers.cfm?abstract_id=1662374.

Breeding, Marshall. 2011. "Automation Marketplace 2011: The New Frontier." *Library Journal* 136 (no. 6): 24–34. www.libraryjournal.com/lj/home/889533-264/automation_marketplace_2011_the_new.html.csp.

Cockroft, Adrian, Cory Hicks, and Greg Orzell. 2011. "Lessons Netflix Learned from the AWS Outage." *Netflix Tech Blog*, April 2011. http://techblog.netflix.com/2011_04_01_archive.html.

Conry-Murray, Andrew. 2009. *The Public Cloud: Infrastructure as a Service*. Information Week Analytics, September 4, 2009. http://reports.informationweek.com.

Constantin, Lucian. 2011. "Researchers Demo Cloud Security Issue with Amazon AWS Attack." *PC World,* October 26, 2011. www.pcworld.com/businesscenter/article/242598/researchers_demo_cloud_security_issue_with_amazon_aws_attack.html.

Eucalyptus. 2012. "Amazon Web Services (AWS) and Eucalyptus Partner to Bring Additional Compatibility between AWS and On-premises IT Environments." *Eucalyptus News and Events Blog*, March 22, 2012. www.eucalyptus.com/news/amazon-web-services-and-eucalyptus-partner.

Europa. 2010. "Data Protection in the Electronic Communications Sector." *Europa Summaries of Legislation,* last modified May 19, 2010. http://europa.eu/legislation_summaries/information_society/legislative_framework/l24120_en.htm.

———. 2011. "Protection of Personal Data." *Europa: Summaries of EU Legislation*, last modified Jan 2, 2011. http://europa.eu/legislation_summaries/information_society/data_protection/l14012_en.htm.

Fang Liu, Jin Tong, Jian Mao, Robert Bohn, John Messina, Lee Badger, and Dawn Lea. 2011. NIST Cloud Computing Reference Architecture, 28. National Institute of Standards and Technology: Washington D.C. /www.nist.gov/customcf/get_pdf.cfm?pub_id=909505.

Feldman, Jonathan. 2012. "Cloud Calculations." *InformationWeek Reports*, March 2012. http://reports.informationweek.com/abstract/5/8735/Cloud-Computing/cloud-calculations.html.

Fox, Robert. 2009. "Library in the Clouds." *OCLC Systems and Services* 25 (no. 3): 156–61. doi:10.1108/10650750910982539.

Gorham-Oscilowski, Ursula, and Paul T. Jaeger. 2008. "National Security Letters, the USA PATRIOT Act, and the Constitution: The Tensions between National Security and Civil Rights." *Government Information Quarterly* 25 (no. 4): 625–44. doi: 10.1016/j.giq.2008.02.001

Han Yan. 2010. "On the Clouds: A New Way of Computing." *Information Technology and Libraries* 29 (no. 2): 87–92. www.ala.org/lita/ital/29/2.

Jaeger, Paul T., Jimmy Lin, and Justin M. Grimes. 2008. "Cloud Computing and Information Policy: Computing in a Policy Cloud?" *Journal of Information Technology and Politics* 5 (no. 3): 269–83. doi:10.1080/19331680802425479.

Jaeger, Paul T., Jimmy Lin, and Shannon N. Simmons. 2009. "Where Is the Cloud? Geography, Economics, Environment, and Jurisdiction in Cloud Computing." *First Monday* 14 (no. 5). http://firstmonday.org/htbin/cgiwrap/bin/ojs/index.php/fm/article/view/2456/2171.

Leong, Lydia. 2011. "Amazon Outage and the Auto-immune Vulnerabilities of Resiliency." *Gartner* (blog), April 21, 2011. http://blogs.gartner.com/lydia_leong/2011/04/21/amazon-outage-and-the-auto-immune-vulnerabilities-of-resiliency.

Limoncelli, Thomas. A., Christina Hogan, and Strata R. Chalup. 2001. *The Practice of System and Network Administration*. Boston: Addison-Wesley.

Mitchell, Erik. 2010. "Using Cloud Services for Library IT Infrastructure." *Code4Lib Journal* 9. http://journal.code4lib.org/articles/2510.

Moorman, Lew. 2011. "OpenStack Compute Enters Testing Stage at Rackspace." *Rackspace Blog and Newsroom*, September 1, 2011. www.rackspace.com/blog/openstack-compute-enters-testing-stage-at-rackspace/.

O'Brien, Kevin J. 2010. "Cloud Computing Hits Snag in Europe." *New York Times*, September 20, 2010. www.nytimes.com/2010/09/20/technolog/20cloud.html.

Reese, George. 2009. *Cloud Application Architectures: Building Applications and Infrastructure in the Cloud*. Sebastopol, CA: O'Reilly.

Rittinghouse, John. W., and James Ransome. 2009. *Cloud Computing: Implementation, Management, and Security*. Boca Raton, FL: CRC Press.

Schaffhauser, Dian. 2010. "Library/IT Relations: Down the Hatch." *Campus Technology*, November 1, 2010. http://campustechnology.com/articles/2010/11/01/library-it-relations-down-the-hatch.aspx.

Smith, David M. 2010. "Hype Cycle for Cloud Computing, 2010." Gartner. www.gartner.com/DisplayDocument?doc_cd=201557.

Trappler, Thomas. J. 2010. "If It's in the Cloud, Get It on Paper: Cloud Computing Contract Issues." *EDUCAUSE Quarterly* 33, no. 2. www.educause.edu/EDUCAUSE+Quarterly/EDUCAUSEQuarterlyMagazineVolum/IfItsintheCloudGetItonPaperClo/206532.

Velte, Anthony. T., Toby J. Velte, and Robert Elsenpeter. 2009. *Cloud Computing: A Practical Approach*. New York: McGraw-Hill.

Chapter Four

Software as a Service and Platform as a Service

In this chapter we examine three specific forms of cloud computing and virtualization: SaaS applications by library-specific providers, PaaS using traditional server-type hosting, and PaaS using dedicated application hosting. I discuss providers that exemplify each model and evaluate each using four broad criteria: expertise required to implement and manage the service; service complexity, sustainability, and durability; service cost; and service migration and portability.

Before exploring each of these concepts in depth, it is useful to define a few technical concepts:

Containers: PaaS solutions deploy services in a construct called a container or environment. This construct defines the available resources, security, and scalability associated with a service distribution. Although containers may be started, or "spun-up," this does not mean that they are running on distinct server resources.

Deployments/distributions: PaaS and SaaS environments offer scalability and simplicity by bundling services into a package that can be deployed as a whole on the IT infrastructure. PaaS services specifically tend to support the concept of version control in conjunction with distributions, which makes it easy to test multiple versions of the same service.

Development toolkit: PaaS and SaaS services may offer some command line or direct application programming interface (API) access to the creation, deployment, and decommissioning functions of a service. These may be offered through a development toolkit that has been integrated into a development environment (e.g., Eclipse) or distribution platform (e.g., Git).

Elasticity: Elasticity refers to the ability of an IT service to scale up or down in response to demand. Elasticity should be evaluated for both PaaS and SaaS services to ensure that the platform selected is both properly sized and scalable for an organization's size.

Environment: Often discussed in the context of containers, environments define the software stack on which services in a PaaS service run. Environments are typically defined by their scripting/programming platform (e.g., PHP, Java, Ruby) and web server platform (e.g., Apache, Nginx, Tomcat).

Events: SaaS, PaaS, and IaaS services should offer some form of event logging as part of the service. This tends to be a log of the actions taken and system response to those actions.

Plug-in/add-on: SaaS and PaaS environments make value-added services available as resources or add-ons in a pluggable application architecture. Plug-ins are designed to be added to a service with minimal configuration and may include database, messaging, or logging services.

Repository: In PaaS environments, this term tends to refer to software source repositories for developed code. The most popular distribution repository for PaaS solutions explored in this book is Git as implemented on a hosted service called github.

Version control: PaaS platforms tend to rely on version control to ensure the ability to control distributions easily. PaaS providers typically support distribution of a software service via a plug-in to popular version control platforms.

SAAS LIBRARY SOLUTIONS

SaaS solutions are often attractive to libraries seeking to offload the risk, expertise, and management issues associated with IT services and are increasingly popular given the use of centrally managed data sets (e.g., link resolver knowledge base and bibliographic databases). Libraries are turning to cloud platforms for data-intensive and new services such as link resolvers, digital reference services, research guides, and large-scale discovery systems, with slower adoption of complex systems such as online catalogs, websites, and digital asset management systems; in general, the tendency is to adopt SaaS solutions. And although SaaS solutions clearly provide benefits—such as enterprise level IT, fast implementation, and minimized impact on library IT staff—they may be more expensive, offer limited customization (compared to PaaS and IaaS solutions), and feature long-term commitments not found in other cloud service platforms. The SaaS library-specific solutions discussed below reflect these characteristics, which are markedly different from the examples discussed for PaaS and IaaS solutions; for this reason, case studies here are grouped into system types rather than vendor platforms.

SaaS Provider Examples

More so than other cloud solutions in this chapter, SaaS solutions tend to focus on library-specific applications. Although there are nonlibrary-specific services, such as hosted content management systems (e.g., wordpress.com) and customer relations systems (e.g., Salesforce.com), these systems are not as widely adopted as library-specific SaaS services. Many of the services discussed here more closely fit the broad terms *hosted* and *outsourced*; their inclusion here reflects the idea that they are made available without any infrastructure, platform, or application-level management requirements. In general, SaaS is distinguished from PaaS in that it more closely fits the "turnkey" approach to systems development.

A good taxonomy of library system types and vendors can be drawn from Breeding's website survey of library automation (www.librarytechnology.org). Breeding categorizes systems into eleven types: library services platforms, discovery products and services, federated search, mobile products, digital library management systems, electronic resource management support, institutional repositories, OpenURL linking applications, resource sharing systems, RFID systems, and archives management systems. In addition to these, libraries tend to use knowledge bases, digital reference service tools, content management systems, and, of course, subscriptions to a host of aggregated information resources that are delivered in an SaaS environment. This review examines systems from three broad categories: next generation cloud-based ILS, DAMS, and public-facing services.

Next Generation Cloud-Based ILS

It is increasingly common to see ILS vendors advertize cloud computing as a key aspect of their ILS. This may include a wholly cloud-based solution or simply virtualized hosting or knowledge base synchronization. By far the most common cloud feature is the provision of SaaS hosting for traditional ILS catalogs by vendors and ILS hosting companies. Hosting for ILS systems can follow either a PaaS or SaaS model, depending on the division of management tasks between provider and customer. These systems are typically implemented as dedicated machines or on a virtualized server that is accessible only by the service provider and customer. In addition to commercial ILS vendors, there are also cloud-based support services for open-source ILS systems including Evergreen (http://open-ils.org) and Koha (http://koha.org). There are also consortiums that have used the open-source ILS platform as an opportunity to engage in statewide hosting. Of note are the Georgia Pines system (http://gapines.org) and an Indiana consortium of libraries (www.in.gov/library/evergreen.htm) that is using Evergreen on virtualized platforms.

SaaS hosting of traditional ILS platforms is different from the new comprehensive resource management platforms (CRMPs). These resource management systems more closely model a web-service-based SaaS environment. They often feature a shared bibliographic database, emphasize interoperability among systems and data sets, and provide access to both public and staff tools via graphical web services. Key vendors in this market include OCLC (WorldShare Management Services, www.oclc.org/webscale/), Ex-Libris (Alma, www.exlibrisgroup.com/category/AlmaOverview), and SerialsSolutions (Inota, www.serialssolutions.com/en/services/intota). OCLC's foray into ILS and CRMP platforms comes from its long history of providing network-based services for libraries. Its introduction of a cloud-based ILS in 2010 marked a shift from providing elemental services such as MARC record management and authority services to providing comprehensive librarywide services. Recent examples of this service include systems at Pepperdine (Bryant and Ye 2012) and the University of Delaware (OCLC 2012).

Just as the information industry has found considerable value in data hosting and ownership, library automation vendors have found not only that libraries are willing to pay for a managed, cloud-based knowledge base but that this knowledge base can be repurposed for a variety of uses. OCLC's product not only leverages the existing bibliographic and holdings database it has built over the past forty years but also uses community-created programs and externally subscribed data sets to bring together the features of the traditional ILS and the new management demands brought on by electronic resources. The result is a new generation of systems that work only as cloud applications. As our exploration of PaaS and IaaS services shows, shifting away from wholly traditional IT practice to "webscale" means blurring the lines between individual and community databases and data sets, redesigning services to optimize web interfaces, and embracing community-shared content.

Digital Archival Management Systems

Cloud-based digital archival management systems (DAMS) include products such as ContentDM (www.oclc.org/contentdm/), hosted open-source archiving services such as DuraCloud (http://duracloud.org), and DSpace hosting from Open Repository (www.openrespository.com), as well as digital publishing tools such as Omeka (http://omeka.net). As with ILS systems, commercial offerings are available as hosted services but are not necessarily designed as an SaaS platform. SaaS cloud support for these systems has not yet reached the maturity of ILS, CRMS, and other systems, perhaps due to the complexity and rapid evolution of DAMS platforms. At the same time, the DAMS poses challenges for libraries due to its relative complexity. In the DAMS open-source market it has become more common for development communities to publish test platforms using client-based virtual machines. These machine images are typically not designed for production installation because they hard-code passwords and integrate database, administrative, and public service functions into a single virtual machine. They are, however, an increasingly popular way for open-source projects to connect with potential adopters. Systems including Islandora (http://islandora.ca), Archivematica (http://archivematica.org), and DAITSS Digital Preservation Repository Software (http://daitss.fcla.edu) are available as simple downloads and can easily be imported into a virtual machine environment.

As use of digital preservation services has evolved, SaaS options for storage, bit checking, and other preservation services have been developed to help libraries manage digital objects. For example DuraCloud (http://duracloud.net) offers cloud broker, data preservation, data replication, and online sharing services for libraries based on the DSpace and Fedora platforms. Both DSpace and Fedora have built-in services that facilitate integration with DuraCloud.

Whereas DuraCloud focuses on preservation services, other platforms such as Omeka and Viewshare (http://viewshare.org) provide a platform for easy-to-use hosted digital publishing. Available both as a downloadable open-source application and as a hosted SaaS cloud solution, Omeka features storage, multiple publishing sites, predesigned functional plug-ins (e.g., geolocation, social bookmarking,

Google Analytics), and predesigned interface themes on yearly subscription terms. Like Omeka, Viewshare is available both as an open-source platform, called Recollection (http://sourceforge.net/projects/loc-recollect/), and as an SaaS-hosted cloud platform. Unlike Omeka, Viewshare focuses on complex metadata and linked data models. Thus it features robust data import, cleanup, and linking services similar in scope to other products such as Google Refine (http://google.com/refine) or Google Fusion Tables (www.google.com/fusiontables/Home/).

Public-Facing Services

Libraries are increasingly turning to SaaS options for public-facing discovery, reference, and fulfillment services. Discovery platforms such as SerialsSolutions Summon, WorldCat Local (www.oclc.org/worldcatlocal/), and EBSCO Discovery Service (www.ebscohost.com/discovery) offer an integrated search platform that includes cloud-indexed print and electronic (licensed) resources. Although libraries have yet to abandon traditional catalogs entirely, the relative popularity of these new systems poses real challenges to locally managed discovery systems including the OPAC.

In addition to discovery services, libraries are turning to virtualized reference services such as OCLC's QuestionPoint (http://questionpoint.org) or SpringShare's LibAnswers (http://springshare.com/libanswers/) or to statewide services such as OhioLINK's KnowItNow service (http://knowitnow.org). Libraries are also turning to self-service information portals such as LibGuides (http://libguides.com) and are leveraging consumer-grade multimedia services such as YouTube and Vimeo to integrate streaming video into online information resources. By deconstructing a complex information service into SaaS-based discrete components, librarians are able to create complex information services with little overhead. Companies including SpringShare are working to provide a diverse set of web services that fit this approach and could easily fill in the gaps left from enterprise DAMS and ILS. The most common form this approach takes is video-based instruction or tutorials. For example, Loo (2010) created and published a series of video tutorials on doing research using PubChem. The video series was recorded using simple client-based screen casting, is hosted on YouTube, and is tightly integrated into multiple web services on an as-needed basis.

As our review of SaaS solutions illustrates, it is realistic for libraries to assemble an entire IT suite using SaaS components. Each of the services represented in figure 4.1 has multiple robust SaaS cloud options, though options may be limited. It is worth noting that, although there are library-specific commercial providers in this

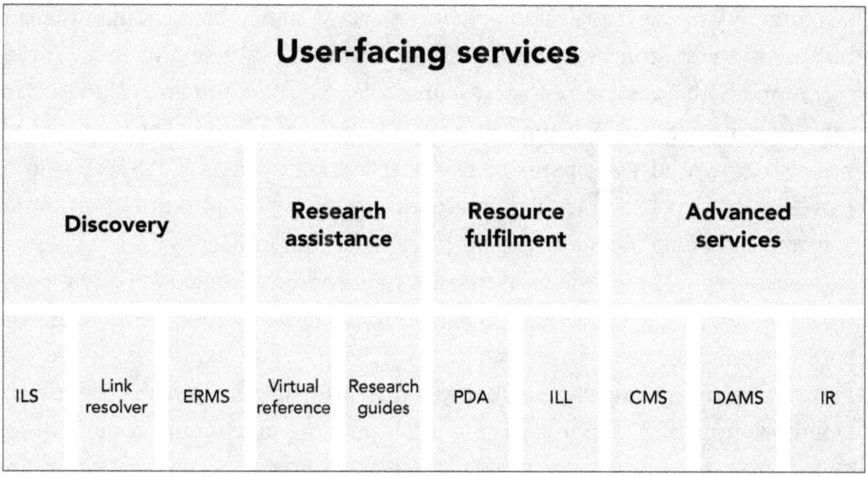

FIGURE 4.1
Public-facing view of library services

space, it is equally common to find open-source SaaS options for specific products. For example, there are hosted open-source products in the ILS, DAMS, and virtual reference service (VRS) product categories. It is less common to find open-source link resolvers and cloud-based discovery services, primarily because these services rely on licensed data sets that are difficult if not impossible to obtain outside of vendor contracts. In particular, these applications that are data-management intensive are good candidates for SaaS approaches because they result in savings at both the IT level and staffing levels in the rest of the organization.

Community Virtualization/Cloud Providers

Cloud hosting for library-specific applications is offered by commercial providers such as Equinox (http://equinox.com) and ByWater Solutions (http://bywaterwsolutions.com) and by nonprofit providers such as Lyrasis (http://lyrasis.org). Many of these providers support multiple systems and open-source platforms. This approach is also being explored by Amigos Library Services, which is piloting a virtualized deployment of the Koha open-source library system with partner libraries (www.amigos.org/node/837). The Amigos project is considering both the technical aspects of virtualized service hosting and the logistics of providing data migration and other ILS-specific services in a hosted environment. Another library cooperative, Lyrasis, provides support for Evergreen, DSpace, and Drupal in a community-based virtualization platform. Lyrasis started its work in virtualized hosting of these services for libraries based on the results of a member survey that found both an interest in open-source software and a need from libraries for infrastructure and hosting support for these software platforms. This work, which has also grown into an open-source site registry known as FOSS4LIB (http://foss4lib.org), has been directed at supporting library adoption of open-source software and filling member demand for specific platform needs.

It is less typical for providers like Lyrasis to provide on-demand or rapidly elastic services. Instead, Lyrasis works with clients to define a customized SLA, negotiate specific access terms and application management agreements, and work with more traditional payment and subscription terms than may be available in other cloud or virtualized platforms. These techniques are much more common from community cloud providers such as Lyrasis. These benefits can be a motivating factor for libraries seeking to leverage cloud-based and virtualized resources to implement new services or manage existing services. Another important advantage of community-specific cloud and virtualization providers of open-source software is improved ability to migrate between providers. For example, FOSS4LIB has four providers listed for the open-source ILS Koha, and Evergreen has multiple providers. Libraries seeking to change providers would likely not have significant issues with data migration and service setup as libraries faced with choosing new systems in addition to new providers.

Issues

Despite the fact that there are a wide range of SaaS platforms for libraries seeking to move to the cloud, adoption of SaaS platforms is not without its own issues. Moving large elements of IT services to SaaS solutions can lead to a fragmented IT environment in which it is difficult to make systems work well together. This can lead to loss of data but more likely to loss of service control and data ownership or access. Likewise, as libraries move toward more data-rich systems, their ability to migrate away from these solutions diminishes. Because there are few standards governing the exiting of a library from these cloud services, vendor lock-in is becoming a significant concern, particularly given the fact that a new breed of tightly integrated knowledge bases and service layers is being developed and licensed to libraries as "black boxes." In this licensing model it is easy for libraries to lose control of the resources that are included and excluded in the subscription. Libraries have become tolerant of this situation, but the growing centrality of subscription resources means that these shifts are poised to have greater impact in the coming years.

Whether cost is an enabling or inhibiting factor depends on a wide range of issues including subscription scale, negotiations, local firm/soft costs, and other IT infrastructure elements. In fact, many libraries are using free services to test and in some cases deploy staff and public-facing services. Although free services are appealing, if libraries adopt them for production-level work they also need to engage in a careful study of the terms of use, exit options, and security system. There are, of course, cloud services such as Facebook, Flickr, and YouTube that are already common in libraries and are known for offering somewhat controversial terms of service to their users.

As libraries opt to spend more resources on outsourced or SaaS services as opposed to developing and maintaining these services in-house, they create an environment in which they may not have the expertise to migrate to new systems or completely capitalize on current systems. There are companies that offer IT support in an as-a-service subscription environment, but these services are often focused on common IT services such as network and client support services. Further, as libraries shift to SaaS solutions they increasingly need monitoring and auditing services that help them ensure that they are both receiving all of their subscribed services and in compliance with organizational policy and legal regulations. As of now there is no service that offers this type of support and few models in the library world that would support such as service. We see some examples of these types of services in chapter 5 as we explore the implementation of IaaS solutions.

Expertise Required

Expertise in adopting and managing SaaS solutions is rather different from that of other platforms. Familiarity with license negotiation and organizational policy becomes a key issue. By turning to a vendor for a wholly hosted service, libraries open themselves up to more legal and privacy issues and need a more solid foundation in negotiating skill. In addition, the key IT skills required for libraries that make extensive use of SaaS solutions include the ability to design and manage metadata and web services that enable system interoperability. This may include working with campus IT to enable system authentication or access and is likely to include staff training and project management tasks. Finally, SaaS solutions often require libraries to have a firm understanding of authentication, access (e.g., proxy access for off-campus users), service management, and problem resolution processes and third-party negotiation.

Service Complexity, Sustainability, and Durability

SaaS solutions are often selected because they offer a highly functional service with simple administrative requirements. By moving the responsibility for system uptime, durability, security, and upgrades to the vendor, the library removes the need to manage these tasks itself. The greatest source of complexity for SaaS systems often comes when trying to connect multiple systems and vendors, or trying to implement new services that leverage the abilities of an SaaS service. In these cases it may be necessary to write data transformation or transfer applications that pose their own complex problems.

Another key advantage to SaaS services is that the vendor providing the service assures their durability. A key risk in this area is the sustainability of a service and the limited number of options for libraries that adopt SaaS services that eventually disappear. Though less common for paid services, free services often change terms or functions and in some cases disappear altogether. Thus libraries should be cautious with regards to using SaaS services that offer no assurance of long-term stability or are still in the development stage.

Service Cost

Calculating costs and ROI for SaaS services can be easier than with PaaS and IaaS services, given the fact that SaaS services often feature a longer subscription term (e.g., year-to-year terms rather than month-to-month terms). However, it can be difficult to compare the costs of SaaS services with those of PaaS, IaaS, and their nonvirtualized counterparts, given the difficulty of identifying hidden or soft costs. Libraries are, however, likely to have expertise in handling these types of subscription models and should be able to project costs over a multiyear period. This longer-term cost projection can be useful in helping libraries decide if an SaaS solution is a better fit than other alternatives.

Service Portability and Interoperability

The ability to integrate SaaS solutions with other systems depends largely on the functions associated with the systems. In larger library-focused SaaS providers it is increasingly common to implement APIs that enable access to data and back-end service elements. Migrating away from SaaS solutions can be difficult because the process of acquiring and managing the data associated with the service can be made more difficult if the organization has lost (or never had) the capacity to work with that data.

PAAS USING TRADITIONAL SERVER-TYPE HOSTING

PaaS offers libraries seeking customized solutions an opportunity to implement web-based services without having to understand the complex inner workings of system administration. Traditional PaaS solutions offer varying levels of access to an IT system and tend to feature a form of LAMP (Linux, Apache, MySQL, and PHP) support. PaaS using a traditional server hosting platform tends to automate system management but often does not include dedicated server access, root access, or the ability to install new system-level tools (e.g., database platforms, scripting languages). Because of this, PaaS solutions should be carefully evaluated to ensure that the services supported match those required and that there is support for system backups, sufficient security measures at the vendor level, and no privacy or data ownership issues raised by using the service.

The server-style solutions featured in this section differ from other PaaS solutions in that they focus on providing limited computational power and storage space but a relatively wide range of IT services. These services often include database management, firewall protection, domain name system (DNS) resolution, e-mail hosting, and other core IT services. These server-based solutions feature a graphical administrative interface (e.g., cPanel) platform that simplifies the implementation and management of web services (e.g., WordPress, database applications, custom-developed PHP, Perl, or Python applications). Often these solutions are based on some form of a LAMP environment or some other common web application framework (Ruby on Rails, Python/Django). These solutions provide a robust IT framework that is best suited to website hosting and customized applications but can also be adapted to run more complex applications such as small-scale library catalogs, DAMSs, and other library-specific services. These solutions can be grouped into one of three types: shared web hosting, virtual private server hosting, and dedicated server hosting. Each of these types has strengths and weaknesses.

Service Types and Providers

PaaS providers offer a good environment for website hosting, content management system hosting, development of web services using specific resources, and ad-hoc use of systems for development or other single-purpose uses. Commercial providers include DreamHost (http://dreamhost.com), HostMonster (http://hostmonster.com), and BlueHost (http://bluehost.com), as well as services run specifically for library environments such as LISHost. These systems are particularly useful for small to medium-sized libraries, libraries exploring virtualized computing for the first time, and libraries seeking to empower staff who have an IT-focused skill set but limited time. The graphical control panel used by PaaS server providers simplifies configuration tasks and eliminates the need to take on infrastructure-level IT management tasks such as operating system maintenance, hardware management, and LAMP stack maintenance. At the same time, it preserves the ability to configure back-end applications. Not every vendor offers these functions, however, and the variation of services and options can make it difficult to select a provider.

Generally speaking, it is important to focus on required features (e.g., hosting functionality, account/data privacy, server location and data center quality, guaranteed capacity, and long-term company viability) and select a solution that fits those needs. PaaS server providers may oversell capacity, assuring customers "unlimited data and bandwidth," but these assurances typically come with caveats and restrictions on content or hosting services (e.g., no streaming of video, no long-term object storage) that reduce the value of these features. Low-cost PaaS providers tend to avoid strict SLA agreements but are likely to provide a "service-level indication" without any clauses for compensation for downtime or any firm guarantee of uptime. More expensive PaaS providers support elaborated SLAs, expand access to the server to include higher levels of administrative access (e.g., root or super-user access), and shy away from overselling capacity, instead leasing a specific amount of disk space, CPU capacity, and application memory to subscribers. The following three sections explore three broad types of PaaS providers in more detail.

Shared Virtual Server

A shared virtual server entitles you to reserved storage resources on a virtualized platform. These providers may feature "unlimited" disk space and bandwidth, but review of their SLAs show that the disk space is limited to the provision of web services hosted on the box and that they do not include backups or storage for file serving purposes. In addition, these providers may restrict CPU use and may not guarantee available memory, making these solutions best suited for website services, small-scale database hosting, or other services that do not consume large amounts of CPU or RAM. Because of these features, shared virtual servers come with the highest amount of risk in a PaaS environment but at the lowest cost. In shared virtual server environments it can be difficult to determine the robustness or geographic/legal location of the data center, and access in these environments is typically limited to web-based control panels or SSH.

Dedicated Virtual Server

A dedicated virtual server is a server to which a user account has exclusive access. Dedicated virtual servers are likely to have a web-based management console and are more likely to allow substantial access to the system for changes to application configuration and versions. At the same time, a dedicated virtual server is likely to be managed at the operating system level by the host company and to feature customized support including tutorials, guides, and even real-time assistance. Dedicated virtual servers include CPU, memory, and disk space allocations along with a level of separation from users not found in shared virtual server environments. As with shared virtual server environments, care should be taken to understand fully the security, privacy, replication, and management features of a dedicated virtual server environment. Legal and technical risks associated with running in a dedicated virtual server environment mean that it is important for providers to have automatic failover capabilities to ensure that a dedicated virtual server is not tied to specific hardware.

Dedicated virtual server environments are capable of running small-scale library-specific applications but are likely too small for discovery or DAMS services that require significant memory and disk storage. Dedicated virtual server environments are best suited for libraries with specific needs not met by hosting in a shared virtual server environment but that also do not want the cost or expertise requirements that come with dedicated server or IaaS solutions.

Dedicated Physical Server

Dedicated physical servers more closely match a managed data center model than the other cloud computing and virtualization models discussed in this book. Many vendors offer dedicated physical servers as an alternative for organizations seeking more capacity or isolation but in a managed environment. This management level is likely to include web-based control panels and super-user access to the machine and does have even higher capacity than dedicated virtual servers. The physical isolation is likely to come with virtual network isolation as well, so that one's server is not accessible by other customers in the data center. This can be an advantage if there are significant concerns over security and privacy, but these advantages are most likely outweighed by the risks associated with being tied to specific IT hardware. For organizations seeking the benefits of physical isolation in an IaaS cloud environment, private clouds hosted inside the organization or subscription-based private clouds such as Amazon's virtual private server environment are more robust options.

Libraries may desire dedicated physical servers if cost, subscriber privacy, or other issues outweigh the anticipated benefits of cloud providers. Libraries that want to operate on dedicated physical servers may also want to consider options in which the library purchases hardware and pays a subscription fee for hosting its hardware in a data center. This approach often comes with higher levels of service, which may include forms of system administration for additional fees, but also enables libraries to benefit from robust data center features such as network redundancy, environment quality, and off-site backup redundancy without giving up the benefits of owning the hardware on which their web services operate. This may be particularly attractive if libraries have adopted an IT service that operates on a platform with which they are not familiar.

It is worth noting that other PaaS solutions such as Salesforce, Heroku, or GoogleApps are not included in the three types of PaaS hosting mentioned above. These solutions focus on supporting highly customized information services such as customer management, site publishing, and content management without the overhead of server management tasks. As a result, these features are more scalable than the server-focused solutions mentioned here but require a tighter coupling between application and hosting environment. These PaaS solutions are reviewed later in this chapter.

When you are selecting a provider it is important to look for objective reviews of each company and to choose a provider based on elements important to your local organization. These elements likely include supported server software, platform security, system management tasks, and SLA options. Figure 4.2 provides an initial checklist that can be used to compare PaaS providers. In addition, it is important to compare real-world costs of these solutions, a process that can be difficult given the fact that some providers charge extra for services such as system backup, SSL support, and dedicated IP addresses (see table 4.1 in "Service Cost," below)

Issues

Although server-focused PaaS solutions offer a simple introduction to cloud computing, they may not scale well in large IT environments and, as a result, can pose challenges for long-term use. This section focuses on relatively customizable PaaS servers that feature a fixed capacity along with web-based administrative

Software versions
- Database type and version
- Scripting language type and version
- Ability to install additional scripting language libraries
- Webserver type and version (Apache)

Security features
- Provider-level firewall support
- System-level firewall support
- Presence of other users on same file system
- File system permission control
- Ability to create/manage users
- Ability to delegate access

System management
- Type of database backups
- Type of file system backups
- Methods for restoring data

Service level
- Uptime guarantee
- Methods for contacting support
- Response time
- Infrastructure present to support SLA (e.g., redundant servers, backups, availability zones)

FIGURE 4.2
Checklist for PaaS server evaluation

tools and specialized customer support. In the next section we explore highly scalable platform stacks (e.g., Amazon Elastic Beanstalk, Heroku) that abandon the server model and instead adopt an application-hosting framework. As you might expect, these two types of PaaS platforms are tuned to different IT needs. For example, server-based PaaS solutions work well in generic LAMP environments where scalability is less important than access to an application stack that has certain automated management features added to it (e.g., configuration, backups, security). In contrast, application-based PaaS environments are best suited to highly customized application stacks and development environments. Regardless, server-based PaaS solutions of both forms are not widely supported by off-the-shelf library information systems. Likewise, the fixed application stack and, in some cases, limited administrative access can limit the potential uses of server-based PaaS solutions and may relegate them to testing or small production deployments.

Expertise Required

The expertise required for server-based PaaS solutions varies widely and depends to a large part on the PaaS platform selected and services implemented. This section reviews the top skills required to make effective use of a hosted server-type PaaS service.

Using a web-based control panel. Web-based control panels are designed to support many of the services that can be managed on a hosted site. Two of the most popular platforms are Plesk (http://plesk.com) and cPanel (http://cpanel.com), but there are a number of other solutions.

Understanding DNS. DNS is the means by which server IP addresses are resolved to host names. When registering with a PaaS provider, you have the option of establishing a new domain name or mapping an existing domain name to your server. For libraries operating as part of a larger institution, it is likely necessary to work with organizational IT to associate the IP address of your PaaS server with an organizationally managed DNS server. To do this libraries should identify a PaaS provider that includes a dedicated IP address along with the subscription; this is required only if the library wants to use a domain name that is related to the larger institutions (e.g., myschool.edu) and not an independent domain name (e.g., library.com). DNS is a complex process that includes the ability to create subdomains, redirect traffic based on name configuration, and support SSL certificates. If your institution is looking to provide its own DNS support, a good overview of DNS can be found in Liu and Albitz (2006).

Understanding service configuration. The support underlying server-based PaaS environments makes it much easier to install, configure, and deploy applications. Many PaaS providers support one-click installs of common content management systems such as WordPress and Drupal. Although these features make it easier to get your site up and running, it is equally important to understand where the files and databases are located for these applications and to understand how application upgrades are handled. It is particularly important to understand how a hosting provider supports the addition of optional modules to popular content management systems. This often requires SSH and SFTP access as well as the ability to set user permissions, extract files, and complete other configuration tasks outside of a web interface.

Understanding SSH/SFTP. To take advantage of PaaS solutions, SSH and SFTP are required to transfer files to/from and interact with your server. Selecting a provider that supports SSH and SFTP is important to enable automation, configuration, and transfer of resources. Many sites support some form of SSH but also require additional security measures before they activate this service. When you are selecting a provider, it is worth knowing if it supports multiple SSH accounts and if there is some provision for using firewall restrictions to limit the IP addresses that can SSH to the hosted server.

Understanding databases. One of the most important elements of a web application is its database. Many web services such as WordPress or Drupal require specific database platforms and may require manual interaction with those databases.

When you are selecting a provider it is important to check the database platforms supported as well as database versions and integration with an application platform. It is also important to know if your PaaS provider supports a web-based database administration tool such as phpMyAdmin or phpPgAdmin (http://phppgadmin .sourceforge.net).These tools make it much easier to configure, manage, and back up databases. It is also important to understand size restrictions, database instance restrictions, backup, and restoration methods coming from your PaaS provider. In addition to these skills, an understanding of database design, SQL, and database integration with web services is essential for application development.

Managing firewalls. One advantage of server-based PaaS solutions is that they feature provider-managed security, network, and operating system updates. A good PaaS provider should protect against denial of service attacks and security breaches in permissions and should block access to server ports by default. For libraries seeking to implement services in addition to a traditional web server (e.g., Tomcat or SOLR) it may be important to manage the ports that are open on your server. Though it can be possible to provide access to these other services through the main webserver port (port 80), it may not be possible to configure this in a PaaS environment. In these cases, having access to some form of firewall control in your control panel is useful. Managing firewall rules in a control panel interface is much easier than administering them directly on the server. This comes with the added benefit that, although an incorrectly applied rule can block access to your server instance, it is not likely to block your access to the administrative control panel. In contrast, firewall services administered in an IaaS environment can be more difficult and come with greater need for testing prior to activation.

Service Complexity, Sustainability, and Durability

Because PaaS solutions offer technical support and simplify the implementation and management of web hosting services, they are best suited for simple web-based services such as library websites, content management services, and customized web services. Given their often limited technology stack and largely managed environment, server-based PaaS environments are often unable to serve as a hosting environment for complex services and may not serve multiple applications well. Providers may not allow root user access and support only recurring automated jobs. For these reasons, server-based PaaS environments offer only a limited ability to increase the IT capacity in a library. Further, though often featuring unlimited bandwidth and disk capacity, they often come with restrictions that prevent the installation of library-specific software such as Koha, Evergreen, DSpace, or Fedora.

This issue can be mitigated by subscribing to dedicated physical or virtual servers, but this tradeoff means that libraries often give up access to administrative control panels to get the ability to install and configure their own software. The benefit of these restrictions is that a server-based PaaS environment is the easiest approach to implement for libraries getting started with cloud and virtualized computing.

Careful attention must be paid to the SLA to ensure that the company has a commitment to providing a high level of service. Even uptime guarantees of 99.9 percent still allow 40 minutes of downtime per month. To understand what a company's uptime assurance means it is important to calculate the actual allowed downtime using an uptime calculator (http://easyuptimecalc.com) and to understand fully how service configuration impacts uptime assurance. In server-based PaaS environments it is possible to find site reviews or recommender services (http://webhostingtop.org, http://en.wikipedia.org/wiki/Web_hosting_service,

Things to Look for in a PaaS Contract

Understanding service contracts for PaaS providers is of particular importance because one's web applications depend on the hardware, software, and IT management services provided by the hosting company. Searching for the following items in provider SLA and license agreements may help guide platform selection:

System uptime: What system uptime is assured or indicated? Are there specific guidelines or restrictions to this assurance? Are there contractual dependencies?

Service features: What IT services are provided? Are there restrictions to specific services (e.g., SSH access)? Does the provider specify a means for managing software versions, dependencies, and other platform-specific functions?

Data ownership and privacy: Does the provider give any assurance of data ownership or system isolation? Is the service located on its own hardware, or is it shared with other subscribers? Does the provider have policies regarding the monitoring of subscribers? What legal recourse is provided for subscribers with claims or complaints?

Security provisions: How does the provider assure system security? Which security elements are the subscriber's responsibility? Does the system support encryption at all levels (e.g., service login, service configuration, service deployment)? What response procedures and communication plans are in place to address a breach in security?

www.tophosts.com) that provide information on site uptime not provided by the hosting company. Uptime assurances should be contained in the SLA, where they likely refer to the company's service infrastructure as opposed to your specific application space. In addition to the SLA, PaaS providers may specify other licensing or contract agreements during the registration process.

Service Cost

Two of the key advantages of hosting services are their relative low cost and ease of setup and management. For example, simple web-hosting providers charge five to ten dollars per month with first-year subscription rate discounts. These base charges may, however, mask second-year or ongoing costs and may not reflect advanced services such as SSL or dedicated IP addresses (important for DNS mapping). In addition, automated backups, additional storage space, and other premium services are likely to be additional charges. For this reason, comparing hosting services at a cost level can be difficult and should be approached with a list of required features.

Table 4.1 shows a cost comparison between different types of PaaS providers based on a simple web-hosting platform with limited data and space requirements and support for dedicated IP and SSL. Rows one and two include costs for two web-hosting companies. Row three documents the cost for a virtual server with dedicated memory and hard drive space. Row four shows costs for a dedicated physical server with specified memory, CPU, and hard disk specifications. Row five documents a provider that supports preconfigured virtual private servers in

TABLE 4.1
Cost Comparison of Small Servers from Paas and Iaas Providers

Hosting type	Yearly subscription	SSL support (private IP, SSL)	Total yearly cost
Shared virtual server (Provider 1)	$95.40	$75.00	$170.40
Shared virtual server (Provider 2)	$107.40	$62.40	$169.80
Virtual private server (Provider 2) (256 MB RAM)	$299.40	$15.00	$314.40
Dedicated server (Provider 2) (2 GB RAM)	$1,188.00	$15.00	$1,203.00
Virtual private server (Provider 3) (1.7 GB RAM)	$1,023.00	$15.00	$1,038.00
Virtual private server (Provider 4) (1.7 GB RAM, no reservation)	$702.72	$15.00	$717.72
Virtual private server (Provider 4) (1.7 GB RAM, yearly reservation)	$335.52	$15.00	$350.52

a PaaS environment and was selected to be roughly equivalent to the dedicated private server in row four. For comparative purposes, rows six and seven include costs for IaaS Amazon web service servers. As the chart shows, simple web hosting is much cheaper than reserved, private, or IaaS server platforms. This cost savings comes with limitations such as lack of reserved CPU or memory and lower levels of assured IT service and could feature additional charges for add-on services such as system backups. In addition, important value-added services such as dedicated IP addresses and SSL security can be more expensive and do increase the total cost of PaaS services.

Service Portability and Interoperability

Easy configuration, deployment, and management are important benefits of server-based PaaS solutions, but they often come at the expense of portability and scalability. When selecting a PaaS solution, it is important to understand what system migration options exist and to document the process for implementing your production environment in a selected PaaS provider. These elements include

Creating a Fail-Forward Plan

Having a good fail-back and fail-forward plan is key to taking on the responsibility of managing your own IT services. A good fail-forward plan should include documentation on

- Application elements
- Core application requirements (e.g., Linux, MySQL, PHP, additional libraries)
- Application version and dependencies
- Application backups (e.g., executable scripts, customized files, database files)
- System configuration (e.g., DNS mapping, user account creation)

This documentation should not just be abstract but should include a plan for implementing your service in a new environment. This may seem unnecessarily complex, but if you are depending on a PaaS server environment it is important to be prepared to migrate to a new provider if the current provider has significant technical problems or goes out of business.

system configuration (e.g., users, open ports, DNS settings, application versions), database and file system contents (e.g., exported database files, backed-up file system), and web server configuration (e.g., home directory, virtual hosts). Though some services such as database and file system elements can be replicated using system export and import functionality, other services such as user management, firewall configuration, and DNS service are likely only configured through the managed web portal. Thoroughly documenting these elements and ensuring that proper backups are created are of great help and simplify the migration process. As a result of the limitations associated with hosted PaaS environments, single-application migrations may be fairly easy, but highly customized applications that depend on specific software elements and versions or on multiple configuration elements (e.g., DNS, database, firewall, web server) are much more difficult to migrate when compared to other cloud platforms.

USING PAAS SOLUTIONS AS AN APPLICATION PLATFORM

In this approach to PaaS, services are geared not toward providing a broad web-hosting platform but rather toward supporting a specific technology stack hosting specific web services. Examples include Google Apps Engine, Heroku, Salesforce, and certain elements of Amazon Web Services (AWS) (e.g., Elastic Beanstalk). These services focus on the "single-platform" method, often supporting limited web application frameworks, databases, and database connection methods. Though the IT stack is limited, the service can provide a more robust cloud infrastructure, ability to scale in response to user requests, and ability to integrate closely with a development environment. For example, Google Apps Engine restricts the developer to versions of Java, Python, and Go and further limits development options by supporting only an NoSQL database on its platform. These tradeoffs enable Google to offer a highly scalable service at very low cost to subscribers. Likewise, Amazon Elastic Beanstalk supports limited deployment frameworks including Java, PHP, Python, and .NET and relies on databases and persistent data to run on other parts of the AWS service infrastructure. By supporting a specific type of deployment, Amazon is able to incorporate the benefits of PaaS environments such as replication and automatic scaling in response to service load. Likewise, by supporting a specific approach to packaging and deploying applications, Elastic Beanstalk enables support version control over the application, enabling easy testing and deployment of new application versions.

These features both enable an enterprise level of support for cloud-based systems and pose problems for libraries seeking to leverage them. For example, no off-the-shelf library applications have been designed to run on PaaS application platforms. Although this may change in the coming years, PaaS application solutions are currently best suited to locally developed applications or specific tailored versions of popular applications. This means that, although SaaS application platforms offer enterprise-level support for service replication and scalability and may offer multiple endpoint or availability zones, they also require the developer to work in a rather narrow development environment using a limited suite of development tools and IT stacks. Some PaaS providers including Heroku address this issue by supporting multiple development platforms and featuring prebuilt services to facilitate everything from database integration to messaging and service monitoring. Clearly these benefits come with their own tradeoffs, requiring more configuration and management of the PaaS service.

PaaS Provider Examples

At the time of this writing, there are few library-specific solutions that run on application-based PaaS environments and no applications designed to work by default in an application-based PaaS environment. It is likely that open-source and perhaps commercial systems will migrate to PaaS platforms given the benefits of this IT approach and the current use of many of the same platforms (e.g., PHP, Python, Java, MySQL, PostgreSQL, Oracle). Key products in this area include Amazon Elastic Beanstalk, Heroku, Google Apps Engine, CloudFoundry, and Microsoft Azure.

Amazon Elastic Beanstalk

Amazon Elastic Beanstalk is a service provided within the AWS framework. As of this writing, Beanstalk supports Java, PHP, Python, and .Net applications and leverages the other services in the AWS environment. It uses Amazon computing instances as a distribution platform and supports scaling through multiple-instance levels from micro (1 EC2 Compute Units, 613 MB RAM) to extra-large (26 EC2 Compute Units, 68.4 GB RAM).

Figure 4.3 shows the Elastic Beanstalk management environment via the AWS web console. As with other Amazon cloud services, one of the powerful features of the environment is the ability to deploy and manage resources using both web consoles and command line tools that have been implemented in several languages

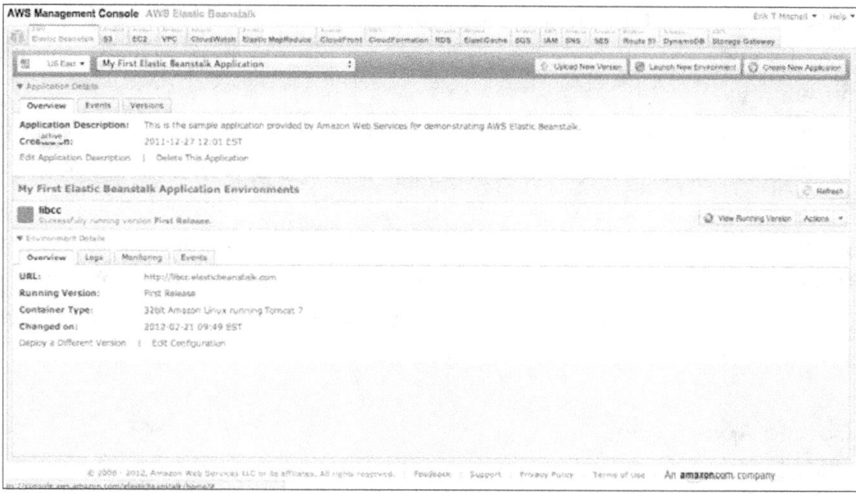

FIGURE 4.3
Amazon Elastic Beanstalk

including Python, PHP, and Java. Beanstalk includes many built-in features such as instance and application monitoring, log file rotation, application version control, automatic scaling, and automatic load balancing. This suite of features is adequate to ensure high-quality service without considerable management tasks and, as our exploration of IT service management principles in chapters 3 and 6 show, delivers many of the key advantages of highly managed systems at a low cost. The Elastic Beanstalk is offered as a managed platform based on other AWS services including the Elastic Compute Cloud, Relational Database Service (RDS), and Simple Notification Service (SNS). This can be good for libraries that already use Amazon services for other cloud environments and have already worked through the legal and organizational issues associated with adopting a cloud provider. On the other hand, Beanstalk is designed around a specific deployment architecture, so systems deployed on it must be set up in a way that requires platform-specific approaches to database management, domain name management, and secure web service implementation.

CloudFoundry

CloudFoundry (www.cloudfoundry.com) is owned by VMWare and supports Java- and Ruby-based environments including Java Spring, Ruby on Rails, and Ruby Sinatra. Like Amazon's Elastic Beanstalk, CloudFoundry supports application version control, testing, and notification services. In addition to the commercial

CloudFoundry system, the organization publishes the CloudFoundry stack at CloudFoundry.org, enabling organizations to deploy the PaaS environment in a private cloud.

Instead of supporting a web-based administrative interface, CloudFoundry uses a client application called Micro Cloud Foundry to allow developers to test and deploy their services. This allows developers to move from testing to production quickly but comes with client configuration and database connection requirements. This is certainly an advantage over other PaaS environments that rely on server resources for a testing or development environment and may be seen as a competitive advantage for CloudFoundry.

Google Apps Engine

Like CloudFoundry, Google Apps Engine (http://code.google.com/appengine/) has both a local testing application and an enterprise deployment platform (figure 4.4). It supports Java, Python, and Go platforms but has customized these deployments to enable close integration with the Google NoSQL database system. Google Apps Engine provides free and premium support levels and bases cost on desired support and service utilization measures. This makes it a good testing and small application deployment environment but also means that libraries may need to review the terms of service carefully if they move from a testing to a production use of the system.

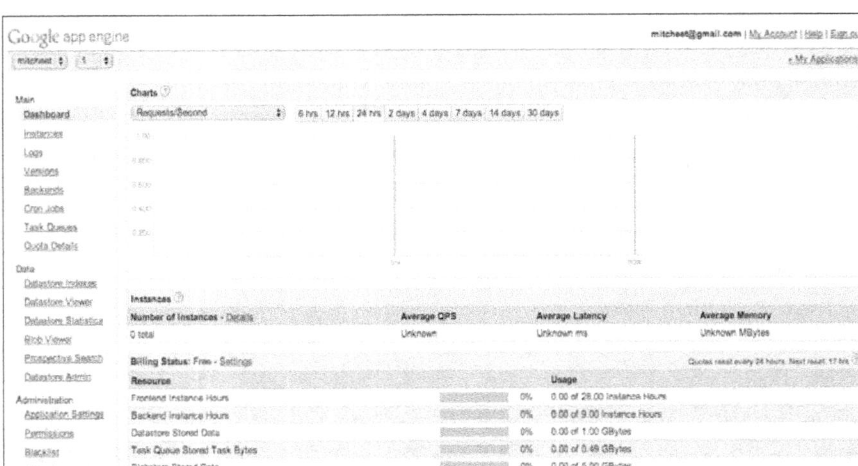

FIGURE 4.4
Google Apps Engine

Google Apps Engine includes tutorials and, like other PaaS environments, supports SSL resolution and custom domain names through URL forwarding. Because it uses customized development and deployment environments, migration to and from this platform can be more difficult than with other solutions. Google Apps Engine recently emerged from beta status, however, and now features SLA levels for paid applications and premier support subscription options. In 2012, Google moved Google Apps Engine from beta to production and released a new beta service called Google Cloud Platform (http://cloud.google.com/), which features Google App Engine, Google Compute Engine, Google Cloud Storage, and Google BigQuery. Each of these four services supports different functions and could be considered to be different types of cloud services.

Heroku

Heroku (http://heroku.com) supports the widest range of development platforms of the reviewed PaaS systems, including Java, Ruby, Python, Clojure, Scala, Play, and Node.js (figure 4.5). Heroku integrates with the Git version control system and uses something called a "dyno manifold" to deploy and run code. Like Google Apps Engine, Heroku features a scalable pricing structure that includes free and premium service levels. Premium features such as SSL, dedicated database support, as well as a host of proprietary add-ons can be added to your service framework in a pay-per-use system. Certain add-ons, such as Amazon's RDS, are free to include

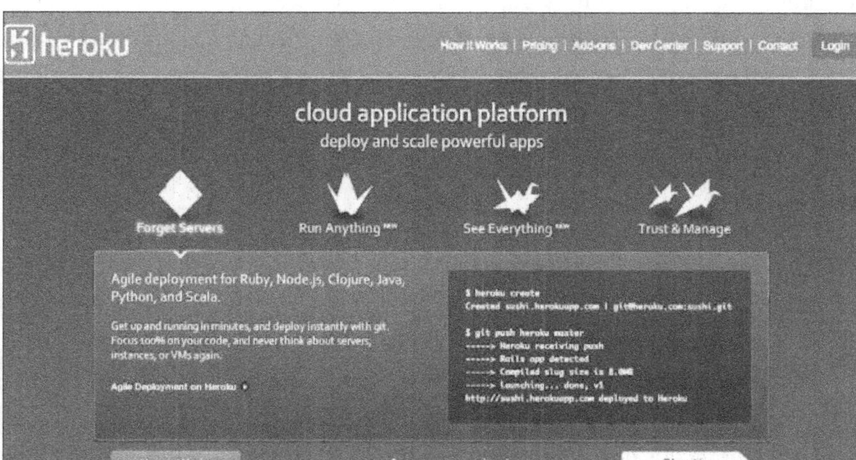

FIGURE 4.5
Heroku

in your application but involve costs and configuration requirements at external vendor sites. The many add-on services allow the Heroku platform to be tuned to fit a wide range of application models, but determining monthly costs and configuring the service can be more difficult than with other platforms.

By using more standardized platforms and an open application publication framework (Git), Heroku preserves the ability to deploy an application or service on multiple providers easily. But this ability depends on designing the application in such a way that static elements such as digital objects and database elements are accessible by all platforms on which the application is deployed. This is likely to require an external managed database platform such as Amazon's RDS and long-term digital object storage in a second cloud provider such as Amazon S3 or RackSpace files.

There have been efforts to deploy library-specific applications on Heroku, in particular Blacklight (http://projectblacklight.org). Matienzo (2012) documented his approach for this process on github.com, and a discussion on the Code4Lib discussion board noted several other efforts on Blacklight deployment on Heroku and Amazon Elastic Beanstalk. Some of the challenges discussed in this thread (Code4Lib 2012) include the need to exclude unnecessary files such as SolrMARC and Jetty to reduce deployment size, the need to host SOLR indexing on a different cloud provider (e.g., Amazon IaaS services), and the challenge that comes with managing gem dependencies and configuring an external SOLR indexing service.

Despite these issues, the testing of Blacklight and the presence of other commonly used web-publishing applications indicate that this type of cloud computing shows possibilities. For example content management applications like WordPress have been customized to work on these platforms (Hoofman 2012; Stein 2011) and could easily fill library website needs. In both cases WordPress installation on Heroku utilizes a plug-in that supports PostgreSQL instead of MySQL but is otherwise unmodified. A key concern with this type of approach is whether a service that has been customized to work on a PaaS platform has "forked," or deviated from the code base to a significant extent. A second major consideration is whether the customized version of the software introduces bugs or future incompatibilities that make support and migration difficult in the future. In the case of the Heroku-customized WordPress application, only a simple plug-in is required to modify the service, and it is possible that library IT departments could find monitoring this one customization worth the increased security and scalability that comes with the adoption of a dedicated PaaS platform.

RedHat OpenShift

OpenShift is Red Hat's PaaS (https://openshift.redhat.com) environment (figure 4.6). It provides support for Java, Ruby, PHP, Perl, and Python applications and JavaScript frameworks including Node.js. OpenShift provides command line tools, REST-based APIs, Git integration, and a browser-based console to configure, deploy, and manage applications. OpenShift also supports cloud-based server creation and management using the AWS platform.

Much like the other PaaS platforms reviewed, OpenShift features a customized application management platform that uses platform-specific tools and instructions. Like other PaaS-based application platforms, OpenShift includes a defined SLA (https://access.redhat.com/support/), SSL, application version control, and some form of DNS management. Although OpenShift is a new service, there have

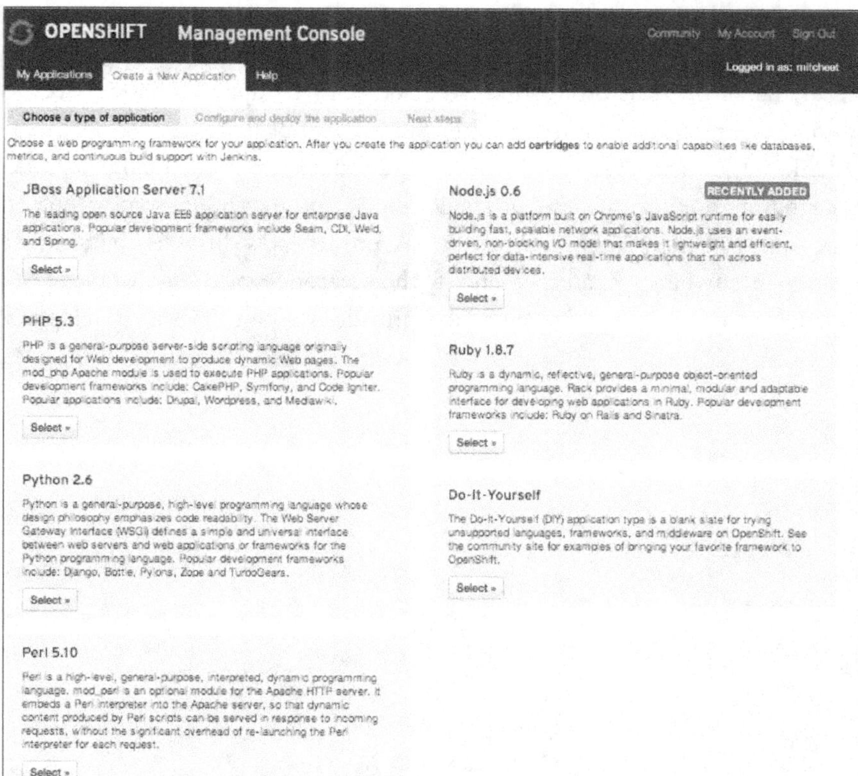

FIGURE 4.6
RedHat OpenShift (Courtesy of Red Hat, Inc.)

been efforts to implement library domain applications using its infrastructure. Van Hooland and Wierckx (2011) have deployed Collective Access (http://collectiveaccess.org) using the OpenShift free tier, which supports an application size of 500 MB and an internally hosted MySQL database. Detailed instructions on the deployment process have been written up by De Wilde (2011) and illustrate some of the modifications commonly required in PaaS deployments of applications developed for traditional IT environments. For example, De Wilde's modification of Collective Access involves using specialized tools, specific exclusion of directories and files, and version control management.

Windows Azure

Windows Azure is a PaaS and IaaS service offered by Microsoft that focuses on Windows platforms for web services (figure 4.7). Whereas the other reviewed platforms tend toward platform-agnostic approaches but emphasize web servers including Tomcat, Apache, and Ngnix, Windows Azure provides support for the .NET framework, Microsoft SQL server, and ASP.NET applications. Services are hosted using Microsoft's Internet Information Server platform.

Like other services, Windows Azure supports load balancing, database integration, application version management, and development environment integration. Unlike Heroku, Windows Azure features durable digital object storage, positioning it as an alternative to the Amazon S3 platform that many PaaS providers support. Windows Azure also provides support for SaaS development

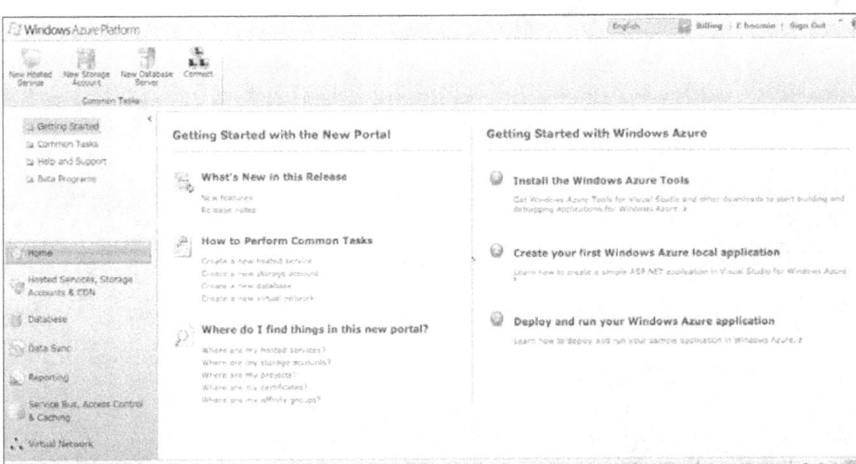

FIGURE 4.7
Windows Azure (Used with permission from Microsoft)

and deployment so that cloud developers can use the platform to provide services to other subscribers. This is similar to the approach of other companies, including Salesforce and Amazon, that support commercial cloud service deployment.

Issues

As the review of PaaS providers shows, the range of services, platforms, and management tools supported varies, and as a result it may be difficult for libraries that rely on off-the-shelf software to leverage these tools. Dedicated PaaS platforms, however, provide considerable capabilities for developers seeking to create and test new applications and likely will be more widely adopted by library system vendors and open-source development communities in the future. In addition to the lack of support of off-the-shelf library software, these types of PaaS systems require new approaches to SSL configuration, DNS name mapping, system backups, and application configuration and deployment. The techniques required often mean that the solutions are more durable than when working with traditional server-based IT approaches, but it can be difficult to learn and incorporate these techniques, particularly because IT departments have traditionally relied on server-based models that more closely match IaaS environments. For these reasons, libraries may find themselves unable to use this type of PaaS platform unless they can dedicate the time required to modify and manage applications so that they work in this environment. Despite this current issue with adoption, dedicated PaaS solutions offer economies of scale, low-cost or free use levels, and a level of durability that can be difficult to achieve without considerable expertise and investment of time and resources using other approaches.

Expertise Required

In addition to the expertise required for server-type management of PaaS applications, dedicated PaaS solutions require specialized knowledge of the system being implemented, familiarity with version management solutions, and an understanding of how to implement and manage database structures in a nonserver environment. For example, Heroku allows one to use several different database platforms, each of which has its own advantages and drawbacks. Being able to differentiate between database and software platforms as well as manage and deploy applications via command line tools can make getting started with dedicated PaaS systems more difficult than working with server-based PaaS or IaaS solutions. As many of the reviewed services point out, these systems are geared toward software developers who need production-level support for their applications but do not have the time or resources to manage the required infrastructure.

Service Complexity, Sustainability, and Durability

PaaS solutions tend to be more complex than traditional IT systems. There are commonly more dependencies required, and each platform takes a unique approach to the deployment, configuration, and management of applications. At the least, a dedicated PaaS environment needs to include an application platform, a persistent digital object storage platform, and a database platform. In a sufficiently distributed architecture, each of these systems should persist without depending on the other. This enables the application to be upgraded, scaled, and redeployed without affecting valuable data and digital objects. One benefit of PaaS application environments is that they tend to include built-in monitoring, replication, and scaling features. Though the default levels of these functions are likely to suffice for most libraries, understanding how to scale these services or reconfigure them to support application deployment on multiple PaaS platforms is necessary for large-scale applications. In addition, for libraries seeking to utilize multiple PaaS providers to make their applications more durable, an external DNS system must be employed to enable easy switching from one service provider to another.

Although there are several issues that libraries must consider when using dedicated PaaS platforms, a key advantage of these systems is their built-in ability to scale and persist across service outages. Amazon's Elastic Beanstalk, for example, includes the ability to scale automatically to handle increased traffic and features multizone redundancy to ensure that an application remains operational even if portions of the cloud infrastructure fail. Likewise, Heroku offers automatic replication and scalability that make it easier to test and deploy system updates. Finally, PaaS environments get their quick configuration speed and flexibility by using shared cloud services. The Zend PaaS (http://zend.com) framework, for example, integrates tightly with RightScale to launch and manage infrastructure-level services onto which are deployed multiple customers. This makes choices about system durability and long-term sustainability more complex and dependent on factors such as local expertise, tolerance for provider lock-in, and ability to implement services on multiple cloud providers.

Service Cost

Whereas PaaS server solutions offer some form of ongoing subscription cost, dedicated PaaS solutions seek to make these service both more affordable and customizable by allowing the subscriber to use only the services required at any given time. In addition, many products such as Heroku, RedHat OpenShift Express, and Google Apps Engine offer free levels of service that may appeal to small and medium-sized libraries. Dedicated PaaS providers tend to charge on the bases of add-ons and IT resources used. It can be difficult to compare costs across providers because each provider uses different measures. For example, Heroku uses a measure of front-end and back-end processes called "dynos" that would be difficult to compare to Amazon's Elastic Beanstalk instances. In contrast, Google has a multifaceted charging model that includes CPU time, bandwidth, and data storage elements. Although there has been some research comparing the total cost of ownership of cloud services, this form of PaaS environment introduces new elements and is in need of deeper exploration.

Service Portability and Interoperability

The complex customization requirements of dedicated PaaS solutions mean that they can be difficult to migrate to new providers. Certain platforms such as Heroku and Amazon's Elastic Beanstalk allow application packages to be deployed on other platforms. In contrast, platforms that use a customized technology stack such as Google App Engine make migrating to another platform difficult if not impossible without additional application development.

CONCLUSION

This chapter explores two broad platform types important to consider when exploring cloud computing and virtualization. The review of SaaS providers focuses largely on library-specific solutions but also highlights SaaS services for broader information uses. Providers such as WordPress and Salesforce may very well be suitable solutions for libraries but should be considered within the overall IT framework required. Indeed, if libraries are seeking to use SaaS solutions to replace all of their information service infrastructure, these options should be considered as ways of bridging the gap between library-specific and general web-based information services. At the very least, however, libraries that turn to SaaS solutions need to consider how they plan to monitor these services, manage contact and access information, and prepare for migration away from SaaS providers.

This chapter also explores two forms of PaaS solutions—server based and application based. Both solutions are excellent choices for locally developed or industry-standard applications but pose challenges for traditional library applications. Server-based PaaS platforms are largely designed to fit the needs of small and medium-sized users, and application-based platforms are designed to be transparent and highly available.

REFERENCES

Bryant, Sally, and Grace Ye. 2012. "Implementing OCLC's WMS (Web-Scale Management Services) Circulation at Pepperdine University." *Journal of Access Services* 9 (no. 1): 1–17. doi:10.1080/15367967.2011.629921.

Code4Lib. 2012. "Anyone Implementing Common LIS Applications on PaaS Providers?" Code4Lib Listserv archive, March 29, 2012. http://serials.infomotions.com/code4lib/archive/2012/201203/0983.html.

De Wilde, Max. 2012. "Collective Access on Red Hat OpenShift." http://homepages.ulb.ac.be/~svhoolan/redhat_ca_install.pdf.

Hoofman, Matt. 2012. "Wordpress-Heroku." https://github.com/mhoofman/wordpress-heroku.

Liu, Cricket, and Paul Albitz. 2006. *DNS and Bind.* Sebastopol, CA: O'Reilly.

Loo, Jeffery. 2010. "Library Instruction through Online Video and Social Media." Chemistry and Chemical Engineering Library, University of California, Berkeley, last modified July 16, 2010. www.lib.berkeley.edu/CHEM/instruction/video/index.htm.

Matienzo, Mark A. 2012. "Blacklight on Heroku." https://github.com/projectblacklight/blacklight/wiki/Blacklight-on-Heroku.

OCLC. 2012. "University of Delaware Chooses OCLC Worldshare." OCLC press release, January 18. www.oclc.org/news/releases/2012/20125.htm.

Stein, T. J. 2011. "Running WordPress on Heroku + Amazon RDS." http://tjstein.com/2011/09/running-wordpress-on-heroku-and-amazon-rds/.

Van Hooland, Seth, and Bram Wierckx. 2011. Open Source Software Platform Collective Access as a Service Solution." DISH (Digital Strategies for Heritage) 2011 conference, December 7, Rotterdam, Netherlands.

Chapter Five

Infrastructure as a Service

For libraries with a background in managing traditional IT resources, an IaaS approach to cloud computing is likely to be a good fit. IaaS providers simplify the process of reserving, starting, and managing IT resources including servers, storage space, network tools, and monitoring tools. This makes it possible for libraries to create an IT infrastructure tuned to specific needs and applications. In addition, these systems often support customization of specific resources such as operating system, application platform, disk space, and memory.

Like dedicated PaaS systems, IaaS systems require a level of investment in the computing environment and have some complicated elements that require familiarity with IT systems and development platforms that are not common skill sets in libraries. With this expertise, the ability to use IaaS resources to create and manage a flexible and robust computing environment can be transformative for libraries seeking new ways to address their IT needs. This also means that IaaS solutions require greater attention to security, backup, and service restoration procedures than PaaS or SaaS solutions and place the burden of ensuring scalability and sustainability on the library rather than the cloud service provider.

In this chapter we review IaaS solutions from two perspectives: using IaaS resources to replicate traditional service architectures, and using them to create cloud-aware service architectures. Before we explore these solutions in depth, it is worth defining a few generic resource types that are common to each of the IaaS solutions. The following list may be familiar, but here they contextualize the discussion of IaaS examples throughout the chapter.

32 bit vs. 64 bit operating system: These numbers refer to the underlying architecture on which the operating system runs. These different hardware architectures require different versions of the operating system, capable of different levels of CPU and memory management. Many IaaS providers base the type of operating system on the server size selected and use some method to automatically scale a 32 bit system to a 64 bit system. Amazon does, however, support operating 64 bit computing images on 32 bit platforms, making it preferable to select a 64 bit operating system distribution if scaling to larger servers is a potential need.

Application programming interface (API): In cloud environments, an API is a standardized programmatic mechanism for interacting with a web service. All IaaS providers have some form of API and often provide enhanced service and functionality through programmatic tools that implement the API functions. There is some effort to begin standardizing cloud API using open-source approaches.

Backup/restore: IaaS providers typically have some systemwide method for handling server and storage space backups. Some vendors provide a managed backup solution (e.g., Linode); others simply provide cloud infrastructure backup tools (e.g., Amazon).

Bandwidth/transfer in and out: IaaS vendors monitor and charge for traffic to and from server instances. It is becoming less common for vendors to charge for incoming traffic, but all vendors discussed in this chapter charge for outgoing traffic. Some vendors (e.g., Linode) include base data transfer levels with server instances.

Cloud file system: Cloud file systems are differentiated from traditional file systems in that they are accessible via APIs rather than via traditional disk or mounting mechanisms. Cloud file systems may feature automatic replication, version control, and other value-added services that make them more reliable than traditional storage.

Configuration profile: Configuration profiles are sets of instructions that facilitate the configuration and deployment of cloud resources. This is an emerging feature of IaaS providers and is implemented differently in each IaaS solution explored in this chapter. The basic concept is similar to automatic configuration platforms such as Puppet and Chef, except that they tend to be used only during system launching rather than on an ongoing basis.

Domain name service (DNS): DNS is a global Internet application that resolves domain names (mycompany.com) to IP addresses (10.10.10.10). Cloud providers offer DNS solutions that are turned to the specific needs of cloud users, such as multiregion routing.

Endpoint: In cloud computing, an endpoint is the point at which the private cloud meets the Internet. Amazon offers multiple cloud regions, each of which serves as an endpoint for traffic from its internal cloud.

File bucket/container: The bucket or container is a unit of storage related to cloud-based file systems. Files can be uploaded only once identified with a specific bucket or container. Cloud providers may also associate access control with a bucket or container.

Load balancers: Cloud providers often support some automated method for implementing a load-balanced application. Load balancers monitor traffic on a given service and reroute traffic or scale server resources as needed.

Machine images: Machine images are the root of the launched servers in IaaS environments. Some providers (e.g., Amazon) allow users to upload, publish, and download images in a community portal; others (e.g., Rackspace, Linode) offer a smaller suite of vetted machine images. All services offer some mechanism by which customized machine images can be saved to the customer's cloud service and reused or repurposed.

Messaging or queuing service: These services provide independent means for sending messages to users or applications. Amazon offers multiple forms including Simple Email Service (SES) and Simple Notification Service (SNS). Messaging services can replace the need to run traditional e-mail and other messaging services on a machine image.

Mountable volume: Some IaaS providers offer a more traditional form of storage that can be mounted as a disk or volume on server resources. Amazon's form of this storage (elastic block storage, EBS) features user-controlled size, format, attach/detach services, and long-term storage.

Public/private keys: In addition to password-based security, cloud providers may support the generation or use of public/private keys for resource access. Of note, all initial access to Amazon-launched resources is via these keys.

Regions: IaaS providers may offer services in multiple cloud regions. A cloud region should be independent both physically and virtually from other regions in a cloud provider's network but should also be accessible via high-speed private networks for data and service replication. Providers may use region replication as a method to assure a high level of uptime in their SLA.

Security groups: IaaS providers typically offer some form of infrastructure-based security. Some limit this to delegated user access to view, modify, or create IaaS resources; others offer a fully functional firewall service.

Server instance: A server instance is an operational server in an IaaS environment. It utilizes an operating system, storage resource, and CPU/memory resources. It may or may not be located on its own hardware (see discussion of public and private clouds in chapter 3).

Snapshots: Snapshots are common in IaaS environments and set a "point in time" backup of a server or storage resource. In the Amazon environment, snapshots are incremental, meaning that each successive snapshot stores only the changes from the previous snapshot. This speeds backup times and saves considerable storage space.

Virtual private network (VPN): IaaS providers may support the creation of a virtual network that limits access to servers based on IP addresses. Users may want to leverage VPN resources in their organizational environment to limit access to sensitive ports (e.g., port 22—SSH).

USING IAAS IN A TRADITIONAL IT APPROACH

Although considering IaaS from "traditional" and "cloud-aware" perspectives may seem artificial, it provides a means to explore the functional implications of different approaches to IT service management in an IaaS environment. As with the wide range of PaaS platforms, IaaS can include a confusing array of options and certainly requires a close examination of the issues explored in chapters 2 and 3, not least of which are the staff expertise, organizational policy, and legal issues associated with moving to cloud services.

In this section we explore platforms that emphasize the traditional server life cycle model (configure, secure, deploy, manage, upgrade, and decommission). The five examples included here are prevalent in the professional literature but are certainly not exhaustive.

IaaS Provider Examples

There are many public or community cloud providers for IaaS services. This book focuses on three in particular (Amazon, Rackspace, and Linode), but there are a host of other providers including GoGrid (http://gogrid.com), Internap (http://internap.com), and Hexagrid (www.hexagrid.com). There are IaaS brokers and value-added service providers such as RightScale and Cloudability. In the private cloud environment, solutions include Eucalyptus, Cloud Foundry, VMWare, and OpenStack.

Amazon Web Services

Amazon Web Services (AWS, http://aws.amazon.com) is perhaps the best known IaaS cloud provider (figure 5.1). Amazon supports a wide range of services including server hosting (EC2), cloud storage (S3, EBS), service monitoring, notification services (SES, SQS), Relational Database Services (RDS), and DNS (Route 53), and service templating (CloudFormation) and monitoring (CloudWatch). In addition, Amazon provides support for public, private, and community cloud environments

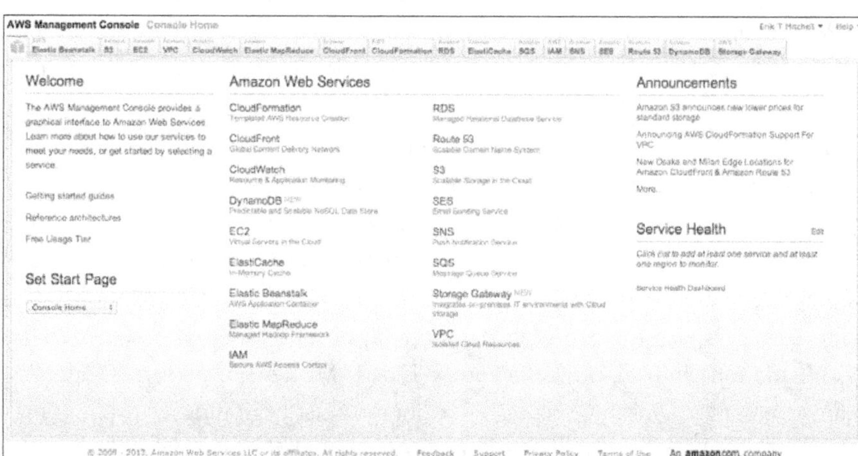

FIGURE 5.1
Amazon Web Services

through its VPC service, GovCloud service, and VPC dedicated instances. Amazon's EC2 service supports a wide range of Windows and Linux server platforms and supports server image import and export functionality. The service features partnerships with licensed server software including Microsoft Windows, RedHat Linux, and Oracle database services to provide licenses "by the hour."

As we saw in chapter 4, these services also lay the foundation for Amazon's PaaS environment, which includes Elastic Beanstalk, RDS, CloudSearch service, and NoSQL database (DynamoDB). Amazon has a considerable lead over many providers in creating a worldwide cloud computing infrastructure, with seven availability zones in Asia, Europe, and the United States. In addition, Amazon provides a service called CloudFront that surfaces network traffic at these nodes, allowing organizations to run complex cloud systems inside a distributed, multizone environment while allowing users to access data from the availability zone closest to them. Amazon's services are often integrated into other platforms. For example, Heroku supports Amazon RDS, and RightScale has adopted Amazon as cloud mirror. The range of features and integration with other providers makes Amazon a good place to start when investigating IaaS systems.

Amazon offers a range of server sizes, server management functions, database services, and disk storage services. Amazon makes servers available using a mix of public, private, free, and licensed Amazon Machine Images (AMI). A robust community has been developed to provide support in this area. It includes free AMI services from organizations seeking to expand the use of the open-source operating systems and paid services from organizations that offer assurances and support agreements along with machine images.

In charging for these services Amazon takes a detailed and evenly split approach, pricing small servers (1.7 GB RAM, 1 CPU) at exactly one-fourth the cost of large servers that are four times larger (7.4 GB RAM, 4 CPU). Amazon regularly lowers cost in small amounts in response to infrastructure savings and does charge different amounts based on selected availability zones. Like other providers, Amazon offers a free service level for new users. This level features a continually operating micro EC2 instance (613 GB RAM, up to 2 CPU units for short bursts) and storage space for one year. Amazon supports a range of server sizes and configurations emphasizing different levels of RAM and CPU resources (http://aws.amazon.com/ec2/instance-types/). For libraries just beginning an exploration of Amazon, small servers ("instances," as they are referred to in Amazon's cloud) are likely to serve as a good testing platform but are not likely to support production services except for low-impact web applications. Amazon instances come with a specified amount of ephemeral storage space that can be expanded or entirely replaced with the use of EBS volumes. EBS volumes are durable virtual volumes that are not permanently tied to machine instances like ephemeral storage is and are easily managed through the web console.

An important strength of Amazon's service is its seven different cloud regions, which make it possible for customers to implement a geographically separated cloud infrastructure. In fact, multiregion replication is a recommended practice for Amazon customers and is often offered as a component of Amazon's managed services including Elastic Beanstalk and RDS. On the other hand, a potential limitation of Amazon is that its services are designed to be implemented in a self-service environment. Amazon does not provide the individualized service that librarians are used to receiving from SaaS providers, and they may find it difficult to get answers to questions and feel confident about adopting a service that lacks a personal level of customer service. In response, Amazon has implemented basic support levels that come bundled with cloud services in addition to premium service levels that operate on a monthly subscription model. The four levels of support include an enhanced SLA that defines support request response time, types of support activities, and scope of systems supported. The Amazon premium support costs, ranging from $49 per month to over $15,000 per month, illustrate why IaaS services tend to be cheaper than PaaS or SaaS services.

Linode

Linode provides an IaaS service similar in scope to many of Amazon's services (figure 5.2). Like Amazon, Linode offers different server levels, from 512 MB to 20 GB RAM. Unlike Amazon, which charges for resources by the hour, Linode charges on a monthly basis. Linode nodes (or servers) come with a specified level of included storage and CPU resources and can be deployed in one of six zones in the United States, Great Britain, or Japan. Linode uses a customized language to deploy and manage servers using the Xen virtualization platform. All Linode nodes include premium support services. Unlike some other IaaS providers discussed in this chapter, Linode offers automated backup and restoration services as well as node-balancing services. By facilitating the process of backup and balancing, Linode helps users capitalize on cloud features with little required knowledge or effort. In addition to backups, Linode offers add-on services that include extra computing resources (e.g., RAM, hard-disk space, bandwidth, or IP addresses). It supports internal cloning of servers and features configuration profiles to help manage server builds.

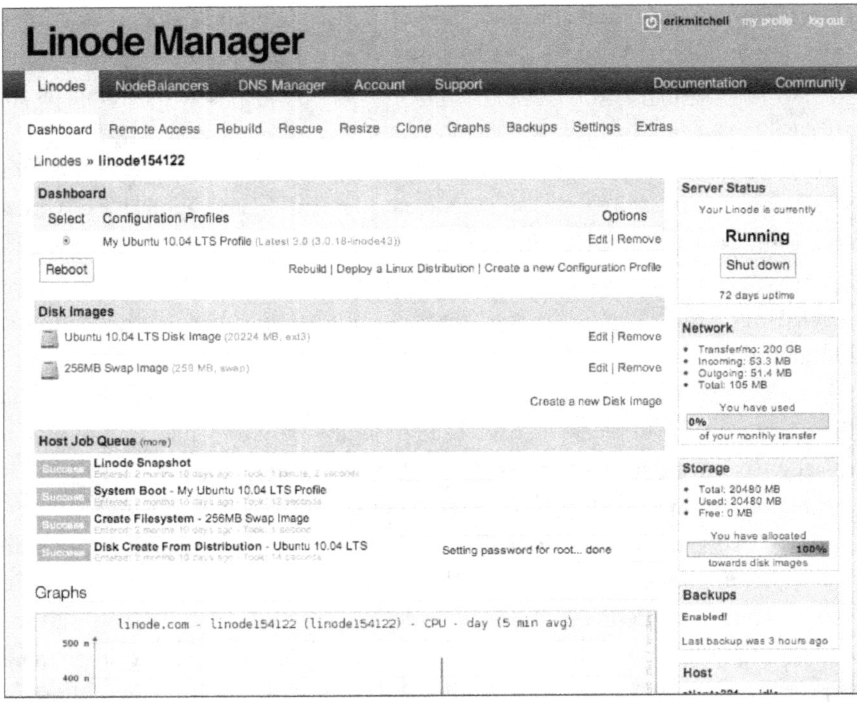

FIGURE 5.2
Linode web console (Courtesy of Linode)

Linode supports multiple users on an account and supports multiple Linux distributions including Debian, Fedora, Ubuntu, and CentOS. Unlike other IaaS services, Linode supports rescue mode booting and other rescue methods. It also focuses on a more limited set of company-managed operating systems than are found on other IaaS providers. The key advantage to this approach is that by keeping the operating system distribution list closed Linode can offer assurances regarding its base platforms.

Rackspace

Rackspace (http://rackspace.com) provides a range of both PaaS and IaaS IT hosting services (figure 5.3). Like Amazon, Rackspace supports several server platforms including Windows and Linux distributions. These cloud servers range in scale from 256 MB to 30 GB RAM and are licensed on a hourly basis. In addition to providing unmanaged server instances, Rackspace provides premium support including managed IT resources, PaaS services including e-mail services and web-hosting services (CloudSites), and private cloud services.

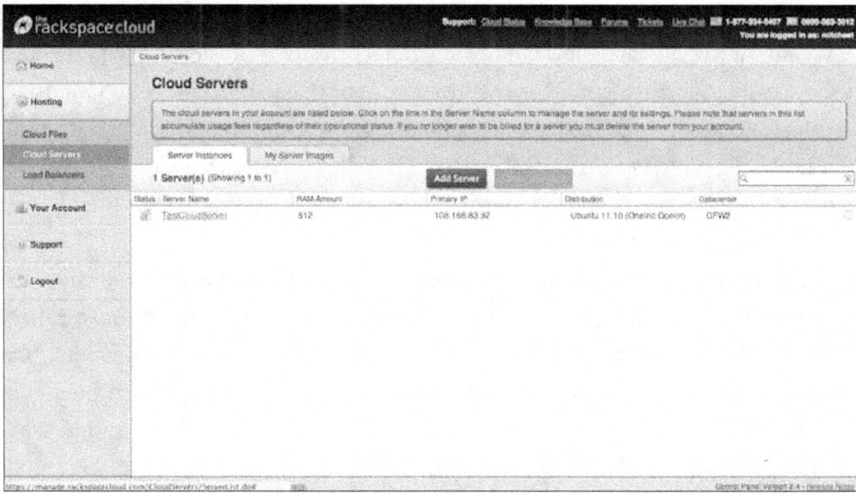

FIGURE 5.3
Rackspace (Copyright Rackspace US, Inc. Used under license)

Rackspace offers a wide range of managed and unmanaged hosting services and features customization options similar to Linode's. It offers a limited selection of machine images but provides support services as part of the hourly server charge and offers a graphical interface for backup configuration and management. Rackspace's support for very small servers (256 MB RAM, 10 GB hard drive space) means that organizations can employ a multilevel architecture that scales servers down when possible to save computing resources. At current prices, the smallest server at Rackspace can operate for approximately $11 per month. In addition to low-cost servers, Rackspace offers managed servers that include load balancing and automatic scaling.

Like Amazon, Rackspace includes server metrics and monitoring services as part of the run-time server costs. The inclusion of an infrastructure-level backup service and built-in support services can make it an appealing option for libraries seeking more control over their server infrastructure but unsure about server management elements such as operating system and backup management.

Private Cloud IaaS Platforms

Along with public, community, and hybrid clouds there are private cloud systems from both commercial and open-source providers that offer organizations opportunities to benefit from cloud computing even if they are not comfortable moving their IT resources to an external provider. For example, Microsoft offers both public (Azure) and private cloud platforms, and Citrix (http://citrix.com) and VMWare (www.vmware.com) offer commercial private cloud systems. Open-source products include Eucalyptus (www.eucalyptus.com), CloudStack (www.cloudstack.org), and OpenNebula (http://opennebula.org). In addition to these private cloud applications, there are private cloud storage systems such as Walrus (http://open.eucalyptus.com) and Nimbus (www.nimbusproject.org) that work directly with private cloud platforms.

Implementing private cloud services is a complex task and requires considerable infrastructure and IT expertise. Libraries may find that their parent organizations are exploring or managing these services or that the scale required results in an overall decrease in cost for the organization. Private clouds may also be a good option for organizations seeking to run their services largely in the cloud while keeping a local backup of resources. Conversely, private clouds can be a good solution for organizations that seek to run their services largely in-house but also want to be able to "burst" into the cloud as needed (see "Cloud Bursting" sidebar, chapter 3).

IaaS Examples in Libraries

Although the survey presented in chapter 2 found that IaaS was not often adopted by libraries seeking to implement cloud solutions, there are a few that have, including Wake Forest University (Mitchell 2010), the District of Columbia Public Library (Tonjes 2011), and the University of Arizona (Han 2010). For example, the Z. Smith Reynolds Library at Wake Forest turned to the AWS platform to implement its entire IT server infrastructure. Amazon services were used to deploy web server, discovery, DAMS, and other services, and PaaS and SaaS solutions were selected for the ILS, OpenURL, and other data-rich services. By using IaaS resources, the ZSR Library was able to implement services based on customer demand rather than on platform support limitations.

This had both positive and negative outcomes: the library was able to increase service offerings but also found itself supporting Ruby on Rails, PHP, Java, and Python applications using MySQL, PostgreSQL, and Oracle databases. In addition, when implementing licensed software, the library found that it had to implement a separate server running CentOS as opposed to its commonly used Ubuntu server operating system. This example illustrates some of the complexity that can come with this approach, but there are also features of IaaS platforms that greatly simplify IT management, including central backup and management services. For example, although the ZSR Library was managing four servers, each with a different configuration, it was able to use the Python BOTO library and built-in Amazon image creation and snapshot tools to implement a consistent and easy way to manage backup and server restoration process for all servers. Likewise, by employing the AWS firewall the library was able to add a consistent level of security across all servers in addition to server-level security measures.

With an appropriate level of support, libraries can manage their IaaS systems in ways that mitigate problems and capitalize on the systems' flexibility. For example, by utilizing server imaging functionality, automatic configuration, and continuous integration services like Puppet (http://puppetlabs.com), Jenkins (https://jenkins-ci.org), or Chef (www.opscode.com/chef/), libraries can create server configuration "recipes" which, when applied to existing or new servers, create all of the configuration dependencies required to ensure easy implementation and ongoing operation of IT resources. Likewise, by using test-driven development, code management such as Git (http://git-scm.com) or Apache Subversion (http://subversion.apache.org), and test and production environments, libraries can ensure that the management of their production services adheres to a high level of IT service management.

Issues

IaaS services enable quick and flexible IT deployments and can be easily seen as the saving grace for IT departments overwhelmed by traditional server acquisition, deployment, and management tasks. IaaS systems are quickly provisioned, configured, deployed, and destroyed and can be scaled based on specific service needs. They enable IT departments to build a data center without the need to support common physical resources including power, cooling, security, and networking. These abilities do, of course, come with complications and difficulties. IaaS services require organizations to take on more IT management responsibilities and technical support concerns. IaaS services also have their own set of legal and organizational policy issues that need to be considered. For example, by taking on the liability associated with operating their own servers, libraries may find themselves needing to be familiar with IT policies and laws that were previously the domain of IT departments. Further, although IaaS services feature great customizability, operating them efficiently requires expertise not often held in libraries.

Perhaps the greatest issue to consider is the capability of your local IT department to manage an IaaS system in a sustainable way. IaaS typically places the burden of configuration, management, and security on the operator and also places stipulations in SLAs that may or may not be achievable given local IT policies. For example, Amazon ties uptime assurances to specific server configuration approaches that add cost and complexity to the local IaaS system. To be protected by Amazon's uptime assurance, an organization must deploy servers in multiple availability zones. For this reason, partially managed services such as Linode, Rackspace, or RightScale may be enticing for users seeking additional layers of IT support.

Expertise Required

IaaS requires nothing short of a fully committed IT department that is prepared to engage with IT resources at a detailed level. Deploying IaaS services requires both an understanding of application development or deployment platforms and a detailed understanding of server configuration and security. Growing a server administrator from existing IT staff is a nontrivial task but can be accomplished with guided training and persistence. Training may include online tutorials or in-person/online fee-based classes. For IT staff seeking to learn more about system administration at low cost or via self-directed means, guides such as Limoncelli et al. (2001) and Nemeth et al. (2006) on Linux administration provide a foundation for budding system administrators.

Effective management of IaaS services requires all of the skills mentioned in relation to PaaS services including understanding application platforms, firewall rules, terminal commands, DNS operations, and control panel management. In addition, an effective IaaS administrator needs a more detailed understanding of operating system functions, user and permission issues, system configuration, and management and system troubleshooting. In addition, many of the skills common to PaaS environments require more detailed familiarity. For example, IaaS servers require command line management of firewall rules, and Amazon features an additional account-level firewall that both adds security and makes configuration of rules more difficult. Many of these processes fall under the heading of "being a good server administrator" and are an important piece of a sustainable IT infrastructure.

Extensive familiarity with IaaS platform. To design an appropriate IaaS infrastructure, it is important that the system administrator be familiar with the range of services available on the IaaS platform. This means understanding the process of launching servers, creating server images, restoring backups, and managing DNS and IP services. In the Amazon environment it also means being able to manage EBS-mounted volumes and understanding the difference between S3-stored and

EBS-stored AMIs. In addition to these basic elements, it is important to understand monitoring services, notification services, Amazon availability zones, and CloudFront and replication options. Although Amazon, Linode, and Rackspace all provide guides and tutorials for this process, it can be difficult to pull all of these elements together. A series of guides and tutorials created from the experience of deploying Amazon services to support Wake Forest University's Z. Smith Reynolds Library can serve as a guide through these elements; these guides are available as a series at http://libcc.org.

Finally, understanding the infrastructure means making difficult choices regarding how to configure and deploy services. For example, choosing to have the IT department run a separate database server, rely on Amazon's RDS, or keep database systems on its application servers is a complex decision with cost, technical expertise, and system sustainability considerations. Likewise, the IT department must decide how to group and isolate IT services on servers and how to manage server configuration and updates as the number of systems grows.

Being familiar with the IaaS platform includes understanding something about the underlying hypervisor that runs the virtualized computing instances. Though an understanding of the underlying hypervisor is not as important as server management, understanding how hypervisors work is an important element of being able to migrate your server image into new cloud environments. At the very least, your IT department should understand the capabilities of the hypervisor and the service's support for downloading server images and volume snapshots. Although it is possible to migrate between incompatible hypervisors, this can be a difficult and somewhat tedious process (Amazon 2012). Still, there are benefits to migration, particularly for organizations seeking to test virtualization systems locally. In certain IaaS environments organizations may choose to run private cloud systems using a common cloud platform or to test exported cloud servers using locally deployed hypervisors.

Understanding backup and restoration. Perhaps the most stressful element of moving to the cloud is making sure that your IT department has a robust backup plan. Without detailed backup and restoration plans, stress levels are high indeed and the first loss of data is disastrous. A backup plan at the least must include tested and easily replicated processes for restoring individual files/folders, entire applications, or entire servers. In an IaaS environment, backup and restoration processes should include a method to redeploy the application or data on a different availability zone or cloud platform, be appropriately secure, and be redundant as required to ensure service sustainability. It is important to know that the IT department is legally obligated to restore or provide access to all backed-up data on demand by legal authorities, so it is good practice to have an automated backup rotation plan that includes backup retirement, specific archiving, and restoration understanding. Several approaches can be employed but are beyond the scope of this book. At the very least, when examining IaaS providers organizations should consider what backup features are included and how they integrate with existing backup practices. Certain providers do feature backups as part of the service offering but may charge extra and may offer only specific restoration services (e.g., restore a complete disk but not retrieve individual files).

Understanding server management, service monitoring, and replication. Server management encompasses server configuration, monitoring, security management service replication, and system updates. At the very least, a server administrator should understand how to create and manage users, how to install and secure applications, how to harden servers against attacks, how to use firewalls as an additional level of security, and how to automate logs and log rotations. Services need to be designed in such a way that they are resistant to configuration atrophy, hardened against attempts to compromise functionality, and capable of being restored or reconfigured easily.

The best way to test the ability to replicate a server is to restore it from scratch using only system backups. Where possible, processes should be automated, and where gaps in service are detected new procedures should be put in place. In the cloud environment it is important that failover plans include the ability to move into different availability zones on a single cloud provider or to migrate to other cloud providers. Services such as RightScale simplify this process by supporting a mechanism to replicate servers across multiple providers. Likewise, Amazon features the ability to migrate services via command line tools. As part of this process it is important to understand what services are available in the case of an availability zone outage.

Another approach to server replication that is gaining support in IT departments is automatic configuration and server deployment that does not rely on cloud providers. Server configuration tools such as Puppet and Chef replace the "golden egg" approach with easily deployed configuration scripts. These scripts document each step in the server creation and configuration process up to and including restoration of data and movement into production. Using such "actionable" configuration documentation, IT departments can save a great deal of time by both restoring service quickly and avoiding downtime by using the configuration scripts to monitor operating servers. Automatic configuration is becoming increasingly common in IaaS providers. Amazon (via CloudFormation), Linode, and RightScale all offer built-in scripted configuration services. Although this may not be the best practice for extremely large IT environments that prefer to host their configuration service outside of a given cloud provider, using the built-in service configuration tools goes a long way toward improving service durability without the overhead of learning and managing another IT management tool.

Another important part of working with IaaS services is determining server capacity needs. All IaaS providers discussed here offer a variety of CPU, RAM, and storage space options, but it may be necessary to test application installs on multiple platforms to find the best-performing and most economical configuration. As an example, Uspal et al. (2011) used a multifaceted approach to test AWS server capacities against comparably sized locally virtualized and physical servers. Although there were variations in server CPU capacity and available memory, all three servers used Intel Xeon CPUs running at approximately 2 GHz and had 6–8 GB of RAM. The researchers used an input/output file testing system named Bonnie++ (www.coker.com.au/bonnie++), MySQL database loading routines, and an ImageMagick (www.imagemagick.org) image-processing routine on 10 million images on all three server platforms as a comparison of server performance. Their tests found that the Amazon server outperformed both the local physical and locally virtualized server in all three tests, with the most dramatic differences associated with file input and output operations. For example, in the Bonnie++ test Amazon servers completed read operations at 92K per second as compared with 38K per second for physical and 18K per second for locally virtualized service. Disk writing and ImageMagick processing showed similar results.

IT service monitoring is another key aspect of efficient service management. Monitoring is increasingly a built-in feature for IaaS systems but often focuses on server monitoring as opposed to application monitoring. Server resource monitoring (e.g., CPU load, hard drive usage, input/output) is important, but so is application monitoring since it allows IT departments to act ahead of application crashes. Large IT departments may have a complex monitoring system, but even small departments need a monitoring solution that ensures services are operational. For organizations seeking a large amount of control, systems such as Nagios (http://nagios.org) provide monitoring for applications, disk utilization, CPU utilization, and a host of other resources. There are also SaaS alternatives to Nagios, including NewRelic (http://newrelic.com) and LogicMonitor (http://logicmonitor.com), that offer similar-scale monitoring services. Nagios is an appropriate service for complex monitoring, but each of the IaaS providers profiled in this chapter offers different forms of monitoring. For example, Amazon monitors server and infrastructure status at different levels and provides a wide range of communication methods. SaaS services such as Monitor.Us (http://monitor.us) provide easy web-based service monitoring.

Ability to budget carefully. Budgeting for IaaS systems is much less predictable than for SaaS and PaaS systems. For example, organizations must be able to predict bandwidth, storage utilization, and CPU requirements for a service and project capacity needs over time. IaaS providers including Amazon offer lower costs for organizations willing to commit for a specified period, so the ability to project resource utilization over one to three years can lead to sizable cost savings. This is a good thing for organizations but requires system administrators to know when organizations need to renew their reserved instance terms. Failing to renew ahead of the expiration date leads to a dramatic unplanned increase in server run-time costs. Though budgeting is often an administrative function, the many moving pieces of an IaaS infrastructure mean that IT personnel are more likely to be asked to determine what it will cost to run an IT service.

Service Complexity, Sustainability, and Durability

One of the main drawbacks of IaaS platforms is their complexity. Libraries often find that an IaaS service is more complex than traditional server platforms, and they often do not have the IT resources to ensure sustainable services. Some keys to avoiding unnecessarily complex services include using a single server platform and application environment, using a single approach for managing all services, and avoiding complex service tuning that does not add sizable improvements. For example, in a traditional IT environment it is preferable to use a logical volume management (LVM) approach that allows volumes to span across multiple disks. By using LVM, IT departments can dynamically add space to volumes without downtime or complex rebuilding of disk space. The major downside of this approach is that LVM requires configuration files and a static set of disks. In a cloud environment it is much easier to image, increase, detach, and reattach volumes. This to some extent mitigates the benefits offered by LVM and has the added benefit of enabling easy imaging, replication, and restoration of disk images without having to keep track of LVM configuration files and volume associations.

Libraries that find themselves administering IaaS environments but are outside of their comfort level can turn to premium support services or seek to simplify service deployment by using a single system configuration and turning to automated management tools. Automated backups, automatic configuration, and regular monitoring and notification services go a long way in helping library IT feel more comfortable with IaaS management responsibilities and can lead overall to a more efficient IT organization. Another approach to simplifying an IaaS environment is to identify services, such as database servers, monitoring services, server builds, or e-mail services, that can be outsourced to a PaaS or SaaS platform. By taking these base-level services out of the mix, organizations can focus on running customized services for only the applications that require them.

Service Cost

IaaS services often cost less than their SaaS and PaaS counterparts, primarily because the latter include value-added services such as IT management, data management, and premium service levels. At the very least, a service cost comparison should include the hard costs of server run-time, storage space, bandwidth, backup, and related infrastructure (e.g., monitoring, documentation, software licensing). A full cost consideration also needs to include hidden or soft costs including those for personnel time, infrastructure management, replication and redundancy plans, and data management. Though planning for and incorporating such soft costs is difficult, even a basic attempt can help organizations fully understand the long-term costs of cloud computing. There are SaaS services such as Cloudability (http://cloudability.com) whose primary focus is on monitoring the use of common SaaS, PaaS, and IaaS services and triggering notifications when services are likely to expire or exceed limits.

Service Portability and Interoperability

Although interoperability between applications in an IaaS environment is less of an issue than in SaaS or PaaS environments, given the control an IT department has over the infrastructure, ensuring IT system portability and interoperability with other systems is a more complex issue. Operations such as firewall administration, user account management, and service management enable application interoperability and data transfer. The larger issue with IaaS platforms is the challenge of moving the entire service to a new platform. This capability has seen increasing support in recent years, and now many IaaS systems support some form of system migration. In addition, services such as RightScale offer configuration management services that help replicate cloud platforms and data across multiple providers. At the very least, a cloud computing plan should include short-term replication and long-term migration planning elements. This may include documenting the server image and data download and redeployment process, server configuration process, and DNS reassignment process.

Comparing Costs across Providers

Expertise, organizational fit, and technical features are important, but a cloud service cannot be competitive if it does not have a competitive business model. Comparing services from Amazon, Linode, and Rackspace actually turns out to be rather difficult, because each service takes a different approach to grouping and pricing IT resources. The comparison offered here uses the service with the most bundled IT resources as part of its pricing model (table 5.1). Unlike Amazon and Rackspace, Linode charges on a monthly level and includes specific data transfer capacity in addition to CPU, RAM, and storage resources. For this reason, two Linode servers are used as template servers for comparative purposes.

Table 5.1 shows the comparative cost for these three services based on a small server template. The table includes two entries for Amazon, the first for an unreserved or "on-demand" instance and the other for a reserved instance. Amazon uses server reservations to allow customers to pay a reservation fee that varies based on server size, server region, and expected utilization (i.e., heavy, light, or medium

TABLE 5.1
Comparison of IaaS Provider Costs

Provider*	Upfront charges	Server costs (monthly)	Bandwidth charges (monthly)	Storage cost (monthly)	Total monthly cost	Yearly cost
Amazon (small)	$0.00	$14.64	$24.00	$0.00	$38.64	$463.68
Rackspace (small)	$0.00	$21.90	$36.00	$0.00	$57.90	$694.80
Linode (small)	$0.00	$19.95	$0.00	$0.00	$19.95	$239.40
Amazon reserved (small)	$62.00	$8.88	$24.00	$0.00	$32.88	$456.56
Amazon (medium)	$0.00	$118.40	$96.00	$0.00	$214.40	$2,572.80
Rackspace (medium)	$0.00	$87.60	$144.00	$0.00	$231.60	$2,779.20
Linode (medium)	$0.00	$79.95	$0.00	$0.00	$79.95	$959.40
Amazon reserved (medium)	$390.00	$23.68	$96.00	$0.00	$119.68	$1,826.16

* Small server = 512 MB RAM, 20 GB storage, and 200 GB data transfer.
Medium server = 2 GB RAM, 80 GB storage, and 800 GB data transfer.

use). For this comparison, reservation fees were used for the U.S. East region and heavy (100 percent uptime) usage. One area of inconsistency in this comparison is with the charges for outgoing traffic. Linode servers include a specified level of data transfer with each server that is not included in Amazon or RackSpace server prices. To compare costs equally, data transfer costs for both Amazon and Rackspace are included at the Linode data transfer levels.

The apples-to-apples comparison in table 5.1 shows Linode as a cost leader for both small and medium-sized servers. In real-world costs, however, libraries may find considerable savings by going with providers that do not bundle data transfer charges with server fees. In fact, in real-world usage over two years with one large and two small servers in operation, the Z. Smith Reynolds Library found that data transfer varied between 100 and 200 GB of data transfer per month and also found that there was more need for storage space and server capacity. Clearly this makes selecting a cloud provider difficult, if only because the growth of services over time can be difficult to map. Our comparison of these IaaS providers found that differences in storage amounts, a lack of specificity of CPU power, and variation in how each company handles value-added services such as system backups, support requests, and server resizing make selecting a provider a matter of local factors. For instance, whereas Linode charges $1 per GB per month for each gigabyte allocated above the included storage amount, Amazon charges $0.10–0.125 and Rackspace charges $0.10. This difference could have a considerable impact in changing the cost for libraries with lower overall outbound data transfer but greater storage requirements for DAMS and discovery services.

PLATFORM-AGNOSTIC APPROACHES TO CLOUD SERVICES

The idea of mixing and matching cloud service providers to find an optimal mix of cost, control, and service quality may not seem particularly groundbreaking. In practice, though, finding the right mix of service outsourcing, local management, and platform-specific migration can be difficult. In this section we explore some areas in which moving to SaaS or specific IaaS platforms can affect service quality and costs positively. Such approaches are not likely to solve all problems posed in the previous sections, but they may be right for organizations seeking a balance between wholly outsourced and internally managed cloud services. As a framework for this discussion, we should remind ourselves of the NIST reference model with its range of service roles associated with cloud platforms, including auditor, broker, provider, and consumer (see figure 1.1). In addition, this architecture explores elements that contribute to a well-run cloud service, including service provisioning and management and service monitoring.

Though it is important to understand each of these roles and to be able to identify service providers that fill them, it is also important to consider what combination of service providers and functions best fits a particular library's cloud service needs. For example, as important as it is to have monitoring, replication, and auditing services, small cloud deployments may be able to utilize a single provider that meets these needs whereas larger deployments may need to seek out providers with more complex capabilities. Here again, the adage "The perfect is the enemy of the good" can be worth considering when bringing together cloud systems to support your information services. In general, a cloud service needs approaches to service provision (e.g., resource allocation and integration), service monitoring/auditing (e.g., service uptime, system security/privacy, service cost), and service management (e.g., staff access, service create/start/stop/terminate, service aggregation) that are easy to use and sustainable.

Hybrid IaaS Provider Examples

Many of the previously reviewed providers including Amazon, Linode, Google Apps, and Heroku offer monitoring, auditing, and cost management services, and it is possible that these services will work well in a limited cloud architecture. There are other services, however, that support cross-platform provisioning, monitoring, and auditing services. This section explores cloud services that can provide libraries with alternative or hybrid approaches to creating a robust cloud-based infrastructure. Three classes of service are of particular interest: multiplatform IaaS solutions, SaaS solutions for effective IT service management, and a mix of cloud resources for point-of-need services.

Multiplatform IaaS Solutions

Unlike other IaaS providers, RightScale focuses on adding management, monitoring, and replication layers on top of IaaS services rather than on providing cloud computing services of its own (figure 5.4). RightScale supports multiple providers including Amazon, Datapipe, Logicworks, Rackspace, and SoftLayer. In addition, it supports private cloud management through support for CloudStack and Eucalyptus systems. RightScale adds value to IaaS providers by providing

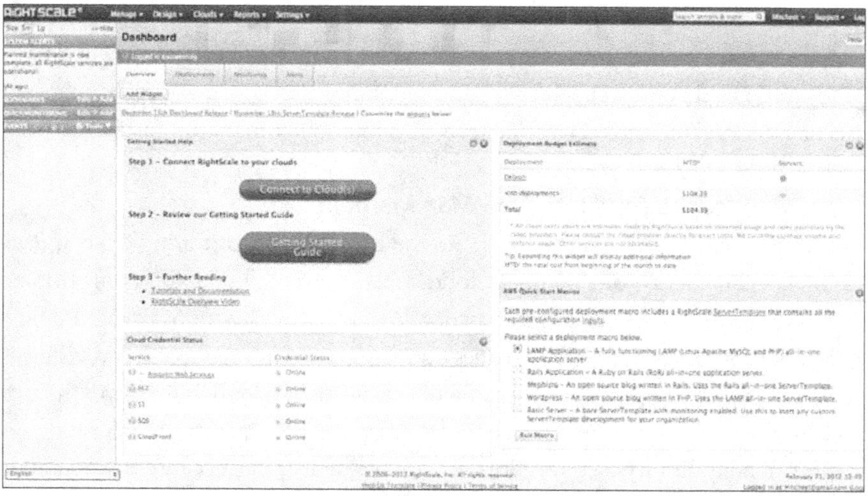

FIGURE 5.4
RightScale (2006–2012 RightScale, Inc. All rights reserved)

a platform for server creation, configuration, deployment, management, and destruction. Its configuration system, known as deployment, uses server templates, customized user data, and scripts to automate server management. Scripts include booting, run-time, and decommissioning functions and enable the automation of complex server tasks.

By providing a configuration and monitoring platform, RightScale simplifies the process of replicating cloud services onto multiple providers. Although this leads to additional costs, it ensures that an organization's service can persist even if its primary cloud provider experiences downtime. By supporting private as well as public clouds, RightScale also enables organizations to alternate between local computing resources and public or community cloud environments. This enables a new level of control for organizations that may want to manage IT services in-house except for those few occasions where additional IT resources are required.

Some providers take on the work of creating and managing machine images for customers but do not do the heavy lifting of service replication in the same way that RightScale does. For example, JumpBox (http://jumpbox.com) and Hyperic (http://hyperic.com) publish prebuilt AMIs on the Amazon platform. These prebuilt servers are designed to be run with minimal configuration while providing monitoring and configuration management services. They can facilitate the deployment of management of services but also require a level of expertise and commitment from IT staff. When handled correctly, they can be deployed as turnkey applications. This requires, of course, that the library maintain permanent data on EBS volumes that they attach to the instances during start-up as well as manage a database server either through Amazon RDS or another managed instance.

SaaS Services to Facilitate IaaS Management

There are SaaS platforms that facilitate the management of multiple SaaS, PaaS, and IaaS providers. For example, Cloudability's (http://cloudability.com) primary function is as a broker and monitor for IaaS services (figure 5.5). Cloudability allows users to register cloud services and then monitors services to provide cost and use auditing services. At the time of this writing, Cloudability supports over seventy-five cloud vendors from a wide range of SaaS, PaaS, and IaaS providers. Unfortunately, library SaaS vendors are not in the list, but because these vendors tend to charge via yearly license models rather than monthly charges there may be little to gain by adding these services.

Cloudability offers both cost tracking and optimization services geared toward finding redundant services and estimating costs for the coming months. The service is useful for organizations that employ a single cloud provider with multiple

FIGURE 5.5
Cloudability

accounts as well as organizations that use multiple cloud providers. Cloudability offers a free usage tier for customers with less than $2,500 per month in cloud expenditures.

Another service similar in function but different in scope is Ylastic (http://ylastic.com; figure 5.6). Focusing primarily on the AWS and Eucalyptus platforms, Ylastic is a subscription service that provides monitoring, backup, service management, and server replication services through an easy-to-use web console. It features management functions in addition to auditing reports, but it functions only with Amazon and Eucalyptus services. As our exploration of PaaS and IaaS services shows, effective management tools that ensure cloud services are durable and easily recoverable are an important aspect of high-quality and sustainable cloud services. Ylastic makes this process easier by providing easy-to-use versions of Amazon services.

Ylastic provides tools that automate many of the complex processes required of Amazon adopters, such as automatic volume snapshots, application monitoring, availability zone migration, automatic image creation, and backup pruning (figure 5.7).

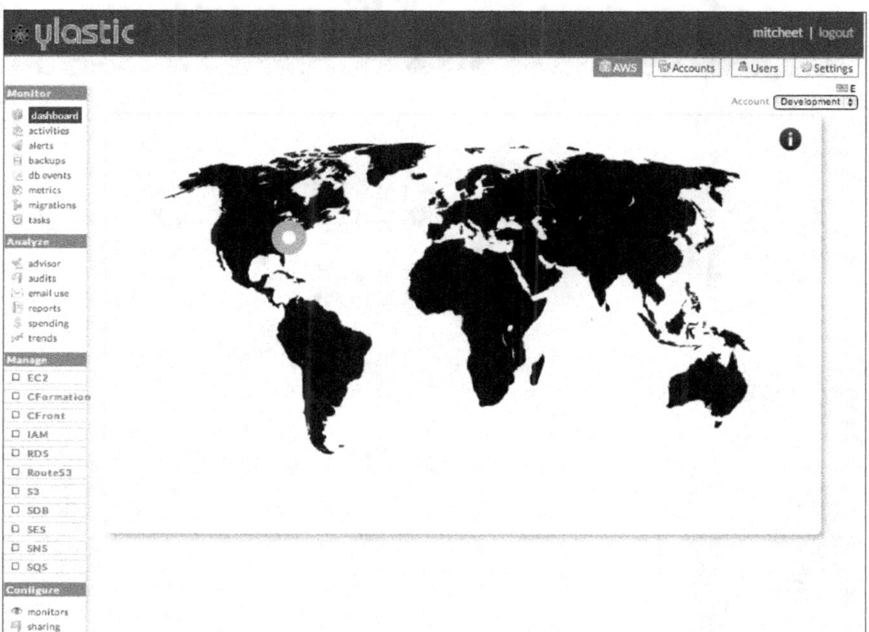

FIGURE 5.6
Ylastic management service

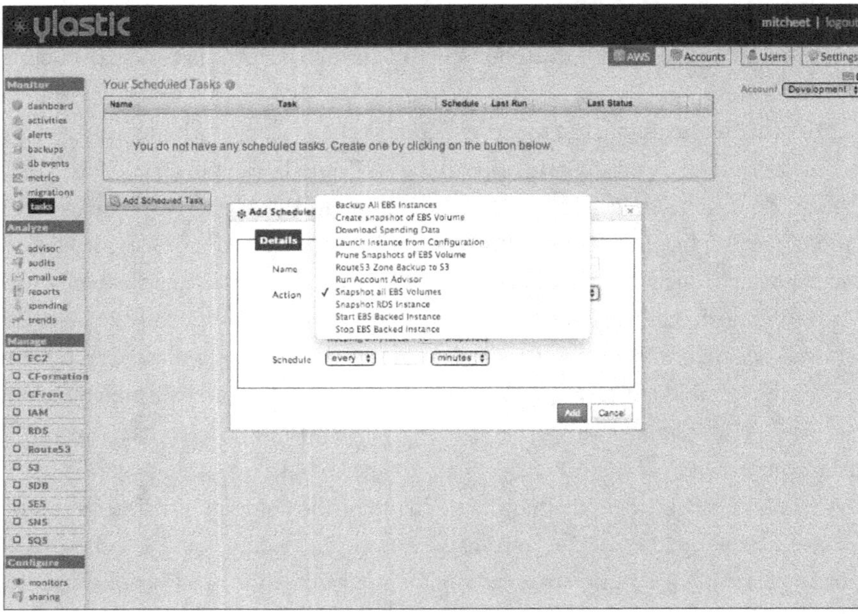

FIGURE 5.7
Ylastic backups

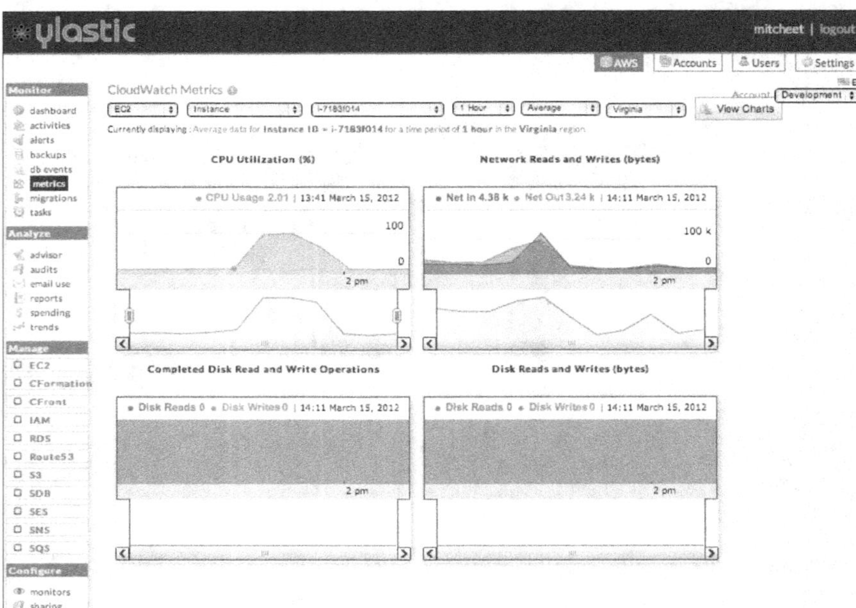

FIGURE 5.8
Ylastic monitoring

Ylastic conducts audits of security, cost, backups, and service redundancy services and monitors service availability. Monitoring includes a focus on service downtime and features multiple notification methods. It also tracks use trends and makes recommendations for removing unused cloud resources (figure 5.8).

Using IaaS for Point-of-Need Service

To this point we have focused on IaaS providers that offer a distinct suite of services. Nevertheless, one of the primary benefits of turning to IaaS solutions is the ability to use distinct elements of the service without large overhead costs. For example, Iglesias and Meesangnil (2010) used Amazon S3 as a storage source for an OAIS-compliant digital object archival system. In combining local and cloud implemented resources they found an inexpensive alternative to SaaS offerings that amounted to a two-thirds reduction in cost per year. Because cloud services involve recurring costs, finding solutions that result in savings of this magnitude can shift the argument away from SaaS solutions. Since this work, Amazon has begun offering an automatic data synchronization service called Amazon Storage Gateway that offers the ability to synchronize locally stored data to Amazon S3 storage automatically.

Whereas Amazon's focus is on simplifying the synchronization of data at the server level, there are also providers that offer client-level cloud-based data and file system tools. Cyberduck (http://cyberduck.ch), for example, is a multiprotocol file transfer and storage mounting service that supports a wide range of cloud storage services including Amazon, Google storage, Rackspace, and Windows Azure (figure 5.9).

Amazon S3 in particular supports advanced file storage service including access control, version control, and event logging. S3 is not a traditional file system, and it can be difficult to use S3 services without a secondary layer or client to facilitate access. Along with server tools that implement S3 integration (e.g., Amanda and KOALA) there are client-centric tools such as CloudBerry (http://cloudberrylab.com), JungleDisk (http://jungledisk.com), and BucketExplorer (http://bucketexplorer.com) that facilitate access to S3 by both implementing FTP, WebDav, or traditional file system volume/disc mounting services and managing services that otherwise can be difficult to manage including file deletion, version control, and access services.

Many of the tools mentioned in this section feature an implementation of Amazon, Microsoft, Rackspace, and other provider interfaces. Although there is a trend for new IaaS providers, particularly private cloud providers, to develop their

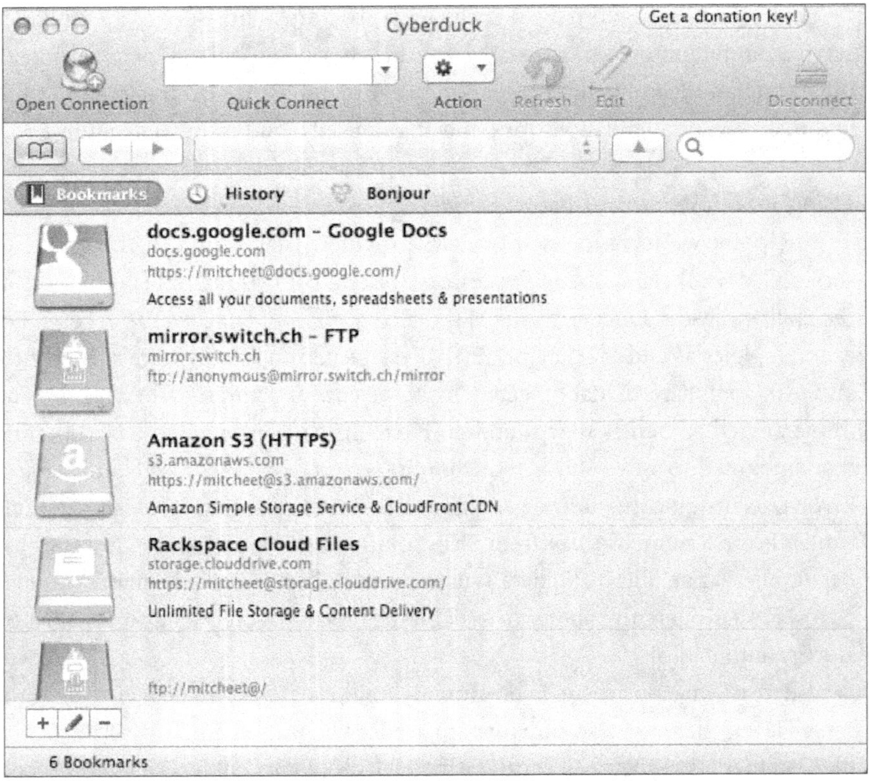

FIGURE 5.9
Cyberduck

command line tools consistent with the commands and parameters of the AWS API toolkit, this approach is far from standardized. As Baun and Kunze (2011, 2) point out, this level of standardization varies across platforms and feature sets. Although Amazon also supports many of the same functions using its web application interface, the command line tools enable automation and advanced access to EBS, S3, and AMI services. We have already explored services supported by Linode, Heroku, Amazon, and Google Apps Engine. Baun and Kunze point to several other PaaS and IaaS tools including GSUtil (https://developers.google.com/storage/docs/gsutil), a toolkit that provides direct access to Google Storage.

The inability of cloud subscribers to use a common toolkit to implement cloud services on multiple providers is a significant problem affecting the long-term sustainability and durability of cloud computing. In response to this need, Christian Baun and Marcel Kunze developed KOALA as an open-source product. The KOALA toolkit both centralizes the management and deployment of cloud services on multiple IaaS platforms using a web service environment and provides a common toolkit library that supports multiple IaaS public and private cloud platforms including Amazon, Google Storage, Eucalyptus, and Nimbus. Unlike RightScale, KOALA is not focused on replicating services across multiple cloud providers but rather provides a common interface to manage disparate cloud providers.

Configuration

Because this section focuses on combining SaaS, PaaS, and IaaS services to create an IT infrastructure, it is worth spending some time exploring which services need to be present in a cloud-based IT environment. These services include application monitoring, automatic configuration, cross-system backup/restoration, IT management documentation, and service and cost auditing. Although it is unlikely that libraries or IT departments are in the position to put all of these elements into place before adopting cloud-based services, they should ensure that these services are in place before moving toward complex IT service deployments in the cloud. For high-quality and sustainable IT service, these aspects must be accomplished:

- Optimize monitoring, backup, restoration, auditing, and service documentation functions; ensure that these services are bulletproof.
- Implement service documentation and ticket management systems on systems separate from the main service system. When production systems experience downtime, having access to documentation and management tools is essential to calm and quick service restoration.
- Design a cloud infrastructure that balances the need to replicate production servers on multiple providers with the need to keep service architecture simple. Although it can be enticing to replicate services on multiple platforms, it is worth considering whether this approach will lead to more uptime or simply more cost and IT management work.

Whereas many providers focus on offering a specific platform or enable wider use of infrastructure level services, a few providers also offer IT management services that automate or simplify the process of working with core infrastructure-level components. For organizations that may need IaaS platforms for specific services, it may be worth identifying SaaS providers for monitoring, auditing, and configuration services so that IaaS platforms can plug into a robust IT infrastructure. These services, including RightScale, Cloudability, and Monitor.Us, do have free service levels, though organizations managing several servers likely need to commit to a premium service level. A complicating factor in this area is that the library IT vendor community as a whole is not included as auditable services in these providers. Despite the inability to audit security and cost for these providers, it is still possible to monitor service uptime and integrate access rules into an IT management system.

By approaching cloud services without focusing on using them as you would traditional servers, it becomes possible to leverage cloud resources in new ways. For example, instead of running dedicated servers for database, web, and other services, consider employing a database or web service that features built-in redundancy and multizone availability. Amazon's RDS, for example, features numerous cloud-based advantages including continuous data protection, automatic multizone redundancy, and automatic management. There are costs associated with running an RDS instance (essentially a small server instance), and your library must run an RDS instance for each database platform required (e.g., MySQL or Oracle), but the quality and stability of the database service can ultimately lead to lower costs and higher quality of service overall.

Issues

Although a holistic or enterprise-level approach solves some of the issues raised by SaaS, PaaS, and IaaS solutions, it also raises issues of its own. First, a multizone or multiplatform solution is likely to be more expensive than other solutions. A multiplatform solution scales very well for small, medium-sized, and large libraries running multiple platforms and application bundles but leads to an overall more complex system with more cost.

Taking a multiplatform approach also requires a high level of IT expertise that may not be common in even dedicated IT organizations. This requirement can be mitigated through the use of SaaS providers for monitoring, auditing, and configuration services but, as with PaaS solutions, adopting a prebuilt infrastructure means that staff must develop expertise in these systems. And though this is a significant issue, it is important to remember that this expertise may lead to cost savings in other areas. By leveraging SaaS infrastructure services to enable the use of PaaS and IaaS platforms, IT organizations can more closely tune platform cost and scale to the information service. For example, implementing an open-source

DAMS in an IaaS environment may be less expensive and offer more future migration options than going with SaaS options. Similarly, though the cost of IaaS solutions may appear high for the first service, with proper use of management tools organizations can adopt multiple IaaS-based services at a much lower cost and with less organizational fragmentation than adopting multiple SaaS services.

Expertise Required

In addition to requiring the skills discussed in the previous sections, personnel expecting to really capitalize on cloud services using IaaS resources need to understand fully system architecture in the cloud. This means understanding how to configure servers automatically, how to set up load balancing services, and how to set up durable database and storage services while capitalizing on creating disposable servers. Coming up with a distributed and durable cloud architecture may seem overwhelming at first, but there are a variety of documented models and setup scripts discussed by the providers discussed in this chapter. In addition, there are valuable case studies from companies such as SlideShare (Mayank 2011) and Netflix (Cockroft et al. 2011) that discuss the process of regular testing of infrastructure to ensure that the cloud environment is durable and secure.

Service Complexity, Sustainability, and Durability

Though IT services in this environment are necessarily complex, the tradeoff for simpler ongoing server management is worth noting. For example, institutions that can turn to a hosted database service (e.g., Amazon RDS) can offload the work required to ensure high-quality uptime for their database services. This may lead to a more complex configuration but also pays off in the form of operational simplicity. For libraries seeking to make IT management an ongoing operation that persists outside of personnel and organizational change, implementing and documenting processes in actionable systems (e.g., automatic configuration tools) as opposed to documentation systems (e.g., wikis, blogs, knowledge management tools) benefit the organization long term.

Although libraries that implement cloud services on multiple providers must also come to terms with the legal and organizational policy issues associated with adoption, it also means that they can realistically look toward their cloud provider solution to be a longer-term solution. With the proper IT and operational support, a multifaceted cloud solution offers better sustainability and durability than any single model, largely due to the fact that the library is in more control of the service and can migrate portions of it without migrating the entire system.

Service Cost

Table 5.2 shows the projected cost of an Amazon service running all applications on a medium- size server (2 GB RAM, 410 GB instance storage, 100 GB permanent storage, 2 CPUs), a MySQL database running on the Amazon RDS service, and the required backups and estimates for data transfer (150 GB per month). To save resources the application server could be configured using the Amazon CloudFormation service and monitored using Amazon and free instance-monitoring tools.

This level of architecture, though not as robust as other solutions, capitalizes on economies of scale with monitoring, auditing, and configuration services within the Amazon cloud and preserves the ability to launch highly customized information platforms. Tables 5.3 and 5.4 provide a high-level cost estimate for Linode and Rackspace running two servers (one database server, one application server) with the same levels of storage space.

Amazon's reserved instance configuration is the cheapest ($1,626), but it comes with the longest agreement—a one-year server reservation. Although the reservation does not require that you run the service, it does lock you into server types. Amazon does have a marketplace in which subscribers can purchase and sell reservations, offering opportunities to purchase and sell instances with other Amazon customers. In contrast, Rackspace is much cheaper than Amazon for on-demand resource costs and is a good fit for short-term capacity. It is worth noting that Linode and Rackspace, though more expensive, do come with built-in customer support levels that fall under "premium" support contracts with Amazon.

TABLE 5.2
Amazon Sample Server Configuration Costs

IT resource	On-demand cost	Reserved cost
Amazon RDS, 10 GB MySQL	$77.86	$21.00
Yearly reservation fee for RDS	$0.00	$195.00
Amazon medium server instance	$118.00	$23.42
Yearly reservation fee for server	$0.00	$390.00
100 GB EBS volumes	$10.00	$10.00
Snapshots with 15% change over month	$14.38	$14.38
Data transfer out	$18.00	$18.00
Monthly total	$238.24	$86.80
Yearly total	$2,858.88	$1,626.60

In contrast, Amazon's storage is less expensive than other services, so libraries seeking a highly tuned environment may find a greater difference in cost as storage demand increases. As this comparison shows, there is no one-size-fits-all approach to service selection, and selecting based on lowest cost alone is difficult given a range of other factors including commitment term, support level desired, balance of on-demand scale versus sustained capacity, and need of specific storage, memory, and CPU resources.

Service Portability and Interoperability

One of the key features of multiplatform services is the ability to move services across providers. Although much has been made of the ability to migrate server images, a properly architected application should be able to be implemented on

TABLE 5.3
Linode Sample Server Configuration Costs

IT resource	Service charge
Linode 512 server for database (monthly)	$19.95
Linode 2048 application server	$79.95
20 GB extra to application server	$20.00
Backup service for Linode 512	$5.00
Backup service for Linode 2048	$20.00
Data transfer out	$0.00
Monthly total	$144.90
Yearly total	$1,738.80

TABLE 5.4
Rackspace Sample Server Configuration Costs

IT resource	Service charge
Rackspace 512 server for database	$21.90
Linode 2048 application server	$87.60
20 GB extra to application server	$3.60
Backup service for Rackspace 512	$4.50
Backup service for Rackspace 2048	$20.70
Data transfer out	$27.00
Monthly total	$165.30
Yearly total	$1,983.60

both PaaS and IaaS platforms. This is not always possible for off-the-shelf library applications, particularly commercial solutions, but it may allow libraries to move common services such as database and file systems to platforms that are accessible from multiple service providers.

CONCLUSION

Many libraries are already leveraging SaaS solutions for common data- and labor-intensive tasks. But because libraries often run specialized and relatively small services, it can be difficult for them to find SaaS or PaaS solutions that fit their needs economically. As chapters 4 and 5 demonstrate, libraries looking to develop their own applications or host relatively common applications such as content management or customer relations systems are likely to find PaaS solutions that fit their needs, and libraries seeking to implement customized library-focused systems such as DAMS or ILS are likely to need SaaS or IaaS solutions. In this chapter, we see that libraries seeking to use cloud computing as a simple disposable service have a variety of options, including application-specific PaaS and managed IaaS. These approaches are transformative in nature and can help IT departments create more durable, economical, and powerful service deployments.

REFERENCES

Amazon. 2012. "Using Instances of Your Virtual Machine in Amazon EC2." *AWS Documentation*. http://docs.amazonwebservices.com/AWSEC2/latest/UserGuide/UsingVirtualMachinesinAmazonEC2.html.

Baun, Christian, and Marcel Kunze. 2011. "The KOALA Cloud Management Service: A Modern Approach for Cloud Infrastructure Management." *Proceedings of the 1st International Workshop on Cloud Computing Platforms CloudCP 2011*. New York: ACM. doi:10.1145/1967422.1967423.

Cockroft, Adrian, Cory Hicks, and Greg Orzell. 2011. "Lessons Netflix Learned from the AWS Outage." *Netflix Tech Blog*, April 2011. http://techblog.netflix.com/2011_04_01_archive.html.

Han Yan. 2010. "On the Clouds: A New Way of Computing." *Information Technology and Libraries* 29 (no. 2): 87–92. www.ala.org/lita/ital/29/2.

Iglesias, Edward, and Wittawat Meesangnil. 2010. "Using Amazon S3 in Digital Preservation in a Mid-sized Academic Library: A Case Study of CCSU ERIS Digital Archive System." *Code4Lib Journal* 12:1-7. http://journal.code4lib.org/articles/4468.

Limoncelli, Thomas. A., Christina Hogan, and Strata R. Chalup. 2001. *The Practice of System And Network Administration*. Boston: Addison-Wesley.

Mayank. 2011. "Puppet in the Cloud." *SlideShare Engineering Blog*, March 2, 2011. http://engineering.slideshare.net/2011/03/cloud-control-puppetizing-cloud-servers-on-amazon-ec2/.

Mitchell, Erik. 2010. "Using Cloud Services for Library IT Infrastructure." *Code4Lib Journal* 9. http://journal.code4lib.org/articles/2510.

Nemeth, Evi, Garth Snyder, and Trent R. Hein. 2006. *Linux Administration Handbook*. New York: Prentice Hall.

Tonjes, Chris. 2011. "Amazon Fail: DC Public Library's Lessons Learned from the Amazon Cloud Outage." American Librarian Association Annual Conference, July 2011. http://connect.ala.org/files/dcpl%20cloud%20computing%20amazon%20fail.pdf.

Uspal, David, David Lacy, and Demian Katz. 2011. "Deploying a Multifaceted Library Support System on the Cloud Using Open Source Components." Montgomery County Community College Technology Conference, October 7, 2011. http://library.villanova.edu/files/4013/3001/4248/Deploying_a_Multifaceted_Library_Support_System_on_the_Cloud_using_Open_Source_Components.ppt.

Chapter Six

Best Practice and Recommendations

In this chapter we discuss ways to get stared with cloud computing by exploring four basic methods of approaching larger-scale migrations to cloud computing that leverage a mix of the platforms and services reviewed in the previous chapters. The four approaches are based on a simple cloud architecture that features an application server, persistent storage space, and a separate database server or database service. The sizes of the server, database, and storage space are not specified; this architecture could scale for small, medium-sized, or large libraries and is capable of hosting multiple applications.

Each approach features common functions, including automatic server configuration, automated backups, a separate database service, a single application server, service monitoring, and cost auditing. Though it is common to find these services in IaaS providers, there the services are not always automated or monitored to the extent needed. Likewise, these services are implemented in PaaS and SaaS environments as well, but there they often focus on distinct applications and cannot be configured to monitor multiple platforms or providers. To stay focused on high-level issues, I do not include in the comparison of approaches the specific functions of monitoring, auditing, firewall services, administrative user access, service growth planning, and budgeting. This certainly does not minimize the importance of designing a cloud infrastructure that includes these highly functional features, for they may be a compelling reason to adopt or reject a platform.

APPROACH ONE: SINGLE-VENDOR CLOUD DEPLOYMENT

A common approach to cloud computing is to select a single vendor and implement a category of cloud services (e.g., all discovery services, all website services) within that vendor's environment. This applies to SaaS, PaaS, and IaaS environments and may be appropriate for specific categories of services. In this case, the single-vendor cloud is used to deploy our hypothetical application/database server environment. Single-vendor implementations can be easier to accomplish and have the benefit of enabling the library to work with a single suite of APIs and administrative interfaces. In the SaaS environment, a single-vendor cloud also likely includes tightly integrated services and efficient data management features. Single-vendor clouds do come with risks of vendor lock-in and service downtime if the cloud service fails, but many vendors have designed multiregion cloud platforms that operate independently, helping customers mitigate the risk of working with a single provider.

As an example, figure 6.1 illustrates an example set of services implemented in the Amazon EC2 cloud environment. This approach uses configuration,

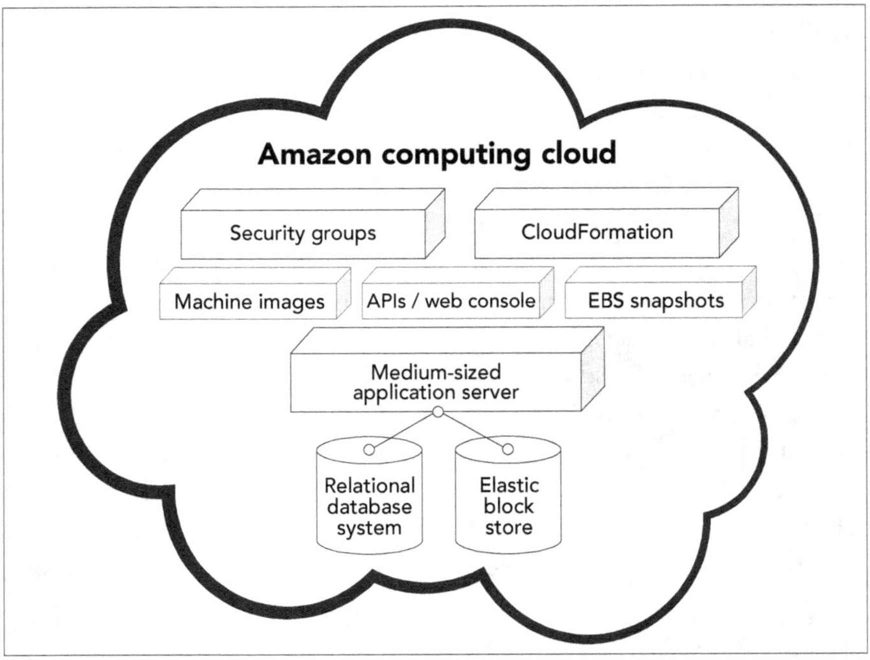

FIGURE 6.1
Sample Amazon server configuration

monitoring, machine imaging, and storage snapshot services built into the AWS platform to manage both the reserved storage space and application server. The Relational Database Service (RDS) is an independently managed service with its own backup and monitoring services. In this example, persistent data are stored as separate 100 GB EBS volumes (e.g., digital images, essential documents, website files) that can be detached from the application server and reattached to a new server if required. Storing important data on EBS volumes rather than on storage associated with the machine instance both makes it easier to migrate this data onto new servers and provides additional levels of redundancy that reduce the risk associated with hosting important files on cloud services.

In this environment, CloudFormation configuration services would be used to document server configuration. The CloudFormation service supports both initialization and setup of Amazon resources (e.g., EC2 instances, EBS volumes, Security Group definitions) and installation and configuration of specific server applications. To accomplish this, the CloudFormation service uses a package management service called cloud-init that is designed to facilitate server configuration during initial start-up. A good "getting-started" guide for this service is in Amazon's documentation on CloudFormation (Amazon 2012). Feid (2012) suggests using Chef (www.opscode.com/chef/) along with CloudFormation to create an automatic configuration tool that is independent of platform and operating system.

Linode and Rackspace offer similar functionality for scripting resource creation and management. Figure 6.2 shows a similar cloud implementation using Linode as the sole cloud provider. Like Amazon, Linode supports multiple cloud regions and has its own customized scripting language, called Lish, to facilitate server management. Linode's monitoring service, like Amazon's, focuses on server health as opposed to application health. Linode uses StackScripts to support automatic configuration and deployment of servers and features version control for scripts to allow easy testing and restoration of services.

Chapter 5 examines the costs associated with a single-vendor model. Tables 5.2 and 5.3 show budgets that generally fit the configurations outlined in figures 6.1 and 6.2. The budgets include a comparison of costs for on-demand and reserved instances but omit charges for services that libraries may want to include from outside vendors (e.g., managed backups, region replication, or application monitoring).

Some benefits of this single-vendor cloud are tight integration between Amazon services; consistent monitoring, configuration, and backup services; built-in ability to scale or replace application server easily without impacting database or digital object storage; and ability to migrate one or more services into new availability

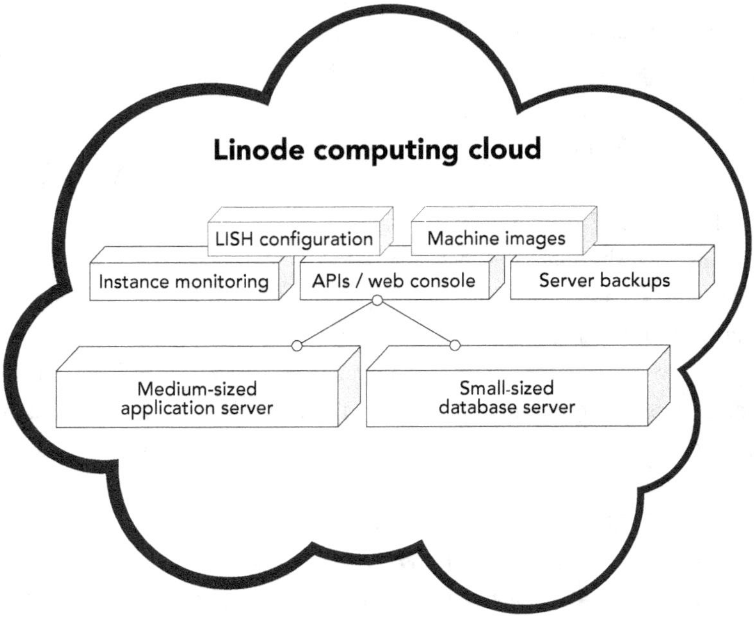

FIGURE 6.2
Sample Linode cloud deployment

zones. In addition, the close relationship between database instance, long-term stored data, and application servers in this approach allows automation of many tasks. For example, it may be highly desirable to configure and deploy application servers automatically but not database and EBS resources. In addition, learning the technical elements of a configuration system pays great dividends in efficient IT service management, documentation, and service quality as the information service matures.

The approach detailed in figure 6.1 also brings technical and configuration challenges. For example, because Amazon does not provide a mechanism for automatic backups in its web console, users must implement a solution using an external vendor or Amazon's command line tools to take regular snapshots of their server resources. Fortunately, because this is a common issue several approaches are available. For customers seeking to keep backup service scheduling on their server, a simple backup script written using one of the available AWS command line tool platforms (http://aws.amazon.com/articles/) works easily. The AWS tutorial at libcc.org (http://libcc.org) features a backup script using the Python BOTO library (http://code.google.com/p/boto/). Likewise, because Linode does not offer a managed database service, an extra server is included as the database server. This actually may be preferable for libraries that use multiple database platforms in their information systems. Although this solution requires that libraries take on database management, it also offloads backup responsibilities. Linode's managed backup service takes care of the backup scheduling and rotation.

Cloud providers do experience occasional downtime, and this is a considerable risk with a single-vendor cloud. There are ways of mitigating this risk, however, for vendors that include multiple independent cloud zones. In the difficulty experienced in 2011, Amazon customers found out how important a redundant and easily replicated cloud infrastructure can be (Cockroft et al. 2011; Tonjes 2011). In fact, Netflix's approach was to build a PaaS environment using the Amazon platform as a way of addressing this issue (Cockroft 2012). In the Netflix architecture, emphasis was put on designing scalability, application publishing, and management using continuous integration tools, database storage using Cassandra (http://cassandra.apache.org), and prebuilt AMIs to deploy operational instances (Chan 2012; Cockroft 2012). One of the interesting outcomes noted in Cockroft's presentation on system architecture was a realignment of IT development away from system management roles (e.g. database administration, system administration).

Another challenge with this approach is the inability to move to a new cloud provider without considerable development time and expense. Although these providers support machine and data exports, the reliance on vendor-provided management services means that migration includes considerable learning and design work. Finally, as our cost analysis shows, relying on a single vendor may push libraries into paying for more capacity than they need in certain areas. Vendors have different cost models for network traffic, storage space, server size, and core versus add-on services. A single-vendor cloud would make it difficult to manage these costs over time as service needs change.

APPROACH TWO: MIXED-CLOUD MANAGEMENT WITH SAAS

Our first approach ties all applications to a single server, requiring the library to manage multiple application stacks and select a server capable of serving all applications. It can be preferable to isolate applications onto separate servers so that downtime or problems with one system do not hinder the others. In addition, libraries may instead want to use a mix of PaaS and IaaS providers to separate out applications on the basis of platform or scalability need.

Although this may lead to a more durable architecture and more efficient use of resources, it can also make it difficult to monitor, audit, and manage these services. To address these concerns there are an increasing number of vendors that provide value-added support on top of IaaS and PaaS services. Some key areas these SaaS services address are service auditing, server and application monitoring, service management automation/simplification, and administrative notification. In our second cloud model, the Amazon cloud described in the first section is retained but another application is deployed on the Heroku platform. The platform may be in use because of Heroku's ability to scale services easily, because of a good fit with an application stack (e.g., Ruby on Rails), or simply to build in a level of vendor redundancy. In this example, database and digital object storage services continue to be offered via the Amazon RDS and EBS services. Figure 6.3 illustrates this deployment and shows how SaaS services such as Ylastic and Cloudability can be used for monitoring, auditing, backup, and replication.

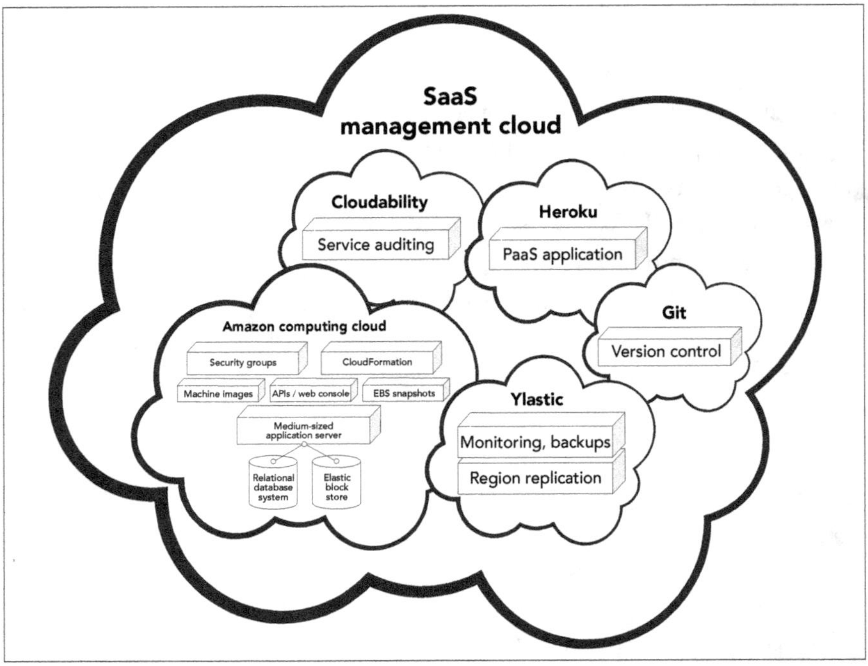

FIGURE 6.3
SaaS-managed cloud computing

This model uses Ylastic to provide application monitoring for both Amazon and Heroku cloud platforms and backup and region migration services for the Amazon platform. Cloudability provides cost auditing for both Amazon and Heroku. By monitoring cost and resource utilization, Cloudability allows administrators to get a consistent cross-provider view of their environment. Although it focuses exclusively on Amazon, Ylastic is able to provide advanced auditing for orphan resources such as unattached EBS volumes. This approach capitalizes on adding value to IaaS platforms by tracking overreserved resources and automating complex functions. For example, our first model highlighted the lack of a simplified backup service in the AWS web console. To address this, Ylastic provides a managed backup service for both EBS volumes and AMI creation services. As figure 5.7 shows, Ylastic offers automated and scheduled tasks that can facilitate server management. In addition, it provides a graphical interface for service replication across multiple AWS regions. Given the fact that Amazon's SLA is based on the ability of subscribers to redeploy services in another region, having a service that facilitates this process could be valuable. The automatic scalability of Heroku, the region replication services of Ylastic, and the resource use notification functions of Cloudability are all features that can save money and simplify IT environments by allowing libraries to scale their services on demand. In a traditional IT model, IT service capacity is centered around the notion of "n+1"—that is, always having more capacity than needed. In a well-managed cloud environment, services can scale up or down based on need or can be replicated into new regions when required, making it possible to provide services "just in time."

Although Ylastic charges for its basic service, some SaaS services do come at no cost for smaller users. Cloudability, for example, provides free cost-auditing services for subscribers with less than $2,500 in cloud expenditures. Likewise, cloud configuration/monitoring services like RightScale and monitoring services including Monitor.Us include a free subscription level. Nevertheless, free services may not be desirable given the lack of local control that often comes with them (see chapter 3).

The benefits of this approach include selective redundancy across multiple cloud providers; automation of infrastructure-level tasks (e.g., backups); clearer understanding of cost and resource utilization; ability to support otherwise unavailable services via SaaS solutions; and automatic scaling, replication, and notification features that allow libraries to move away from the "just in case" models of IT planning to a "just in time" model. There are also some challenges with this approach. The added complexity of using multiple providers needs to result in better service or a more durable or manageable system. Systems that rely on more than one provider to function run the risk of reduced stability and increased downtime as the SLAs of both vendors come into play. There is also a risk with turning key infrastructure functions such as backup over to SaaS options. This creates the same vendor lock-in risk discussed in our first model and requires that IT departments view these services as core elements of their IT infrastructure. For this reason, the services easiest to adopt in this environment are those whose temporary or permanent failure would not compromise the integrity of core library services. Finally, the SaaS services described in this model rely on IaaS vendor APIs and shared keys. Although it may ultimately make sense to use an SaaS service to benefit from economies of scale, it can be equally valuable to invest in developing local expertise for working with the command line tools instead.

APPROACH THREE: REDUNDANT AND SCALABLE MULTICLOUD DEPLOYMENTS

Like our second approach, the third uses multiple providers and SaaS but adds abstracting service configuration and deployment to an SaaS provider. IaaS providers tend to do a good job creating a durable cloud framework but in exchange may focus less on simple IT administration services. Learning the API framework of IaaS providers is useful for ensuring a high-quality cloud infrastructure, but it can be difficult for a small IT environment to learn to work with multiple IaaS platforms using this approach.

Approach three seeks to balance the benefits of using multiple cloud IaaS providers while limiting the challenges associated with managing services without focusing on which IaaS provider runs each service. Two resources discussed in chapter 5 seek to serve this need: RightScale and KOALA. These services use a configuration and resource deployment platform to enable IT administrators to move services easily between cloud providers. This process means that certain services such as DNS resolution and server configuration tools are offloaded to these cloud services, but in exchange RightScale manages replication across multiple cloud providers. Figure 6.4 shows a potential configuration using RightScale to monitor and manage cloud services on Amazon, Rackspace, and a private cloud running Eucalyptus. It also shows the use of Cloudability to audit cost and resource utilization across these providers.

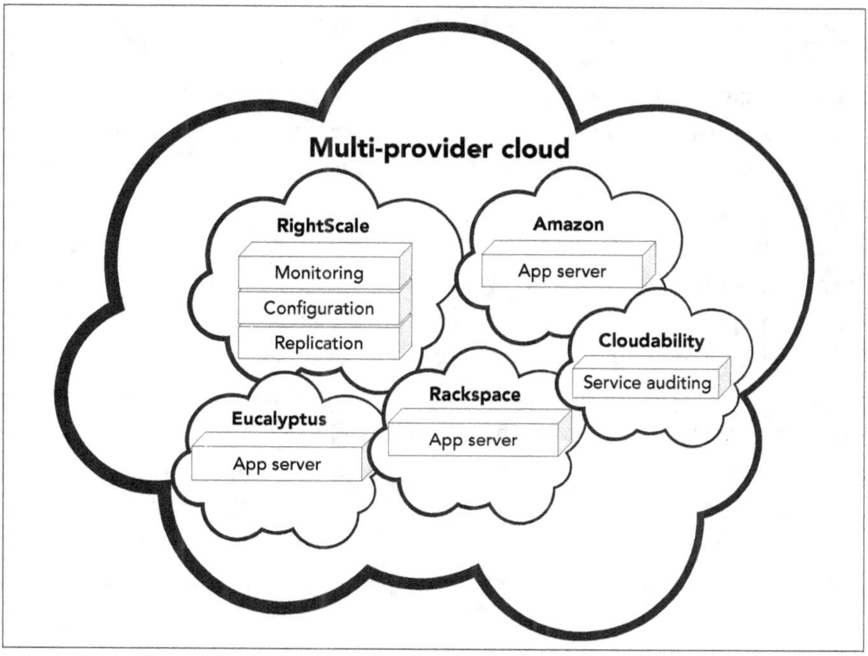

FIGURE 6.4
Multiple managed cloud services

This model is agnostic to the types of services run on each cloud provider but instead focuses on distributed service replication. The model may still use the Amazon RDS service or may use a continual backup and replication service to host the database on different cloud providers. This is made possible through RightScale's use of multicloud templates and images that automatically replicate or back up services onto multiple cloud systems. For example, RightScale publishes a managed MySQL database server that runs on multiple cloud platforms, backs up to Amazon S3 and Rackspace CloudFiles, and includes tools to assist with database recovery and firewall management. In this model the private cloud (e.g., Eucalyptus) may be used as the primary service or simply as a redundant service in case the other providers experience difficulties. This model does not include PaaS providers, but it would be possible to build PaaS solutions into this framework as well.

An alternative approach to this configuration is to use KOALA as the federated system configuration and management tool. KOALA was designed as an open-source product that can be implemented in a PaaS environment using the Google

Apps engine. KOALA focuses on different cloud services and is valuable because it provides a consistent management interface for both public cloud services like Amazon and private cloud services such as Eucalyptus. The KOALA framework would emphasize a common toolkit over managed images and replication services but would provide adopters with a simple-to-use platform that solved the API discrepancies between providers.

The benefits of this approach include the highly distributed use of cloud vendors; automated replication of services and management of DNS that can be tied into monitoring tools; incorporation of private cloud functions; abstraction of server configuration from specific providers; and automatic configuration of enterprise-scale database and application services. At the same time, this distributed vendor model is more complex than the other approaches and may lead to overall higher costs. As seen in chapter 5, many IaaS providers are designing systems that tightly integrate with private cloud platforms through common APIs and cloud bursting functionality. This is a useful development, but libraries without large IT departments or with applications designed to run in traditional server environments may not be able to take advantage of these features.

APPROACH FOUR: DISTRIBUTED SAAS ENVIRONMENTS

The three approaches reviewed above are based on the premise that libraries will turn to PaaS and IaaS solutions for specific services. This is not to say that library-specific SaaS solutions are not yet mature enough for widespread adoption. There are now many options for libraries seeking SaaS solutions for all of their services. Existing vendors are expanding both their use of cloud approaches and their product suites, and new companies have emerged to provide website, virtual reference, media hosting, and other information services. In fact, every key information system including the ILS, DAMS, link resolver, digital reference, discovery, resource fulfillment, electronic resource management systems, and websites are available in SaaS forms. In figure 6.5 a hypothetical library relies on a mix of commercial and consortial providers for system support. In each case, the system is offered in a managed SaaS environment, and the library is responsible for ensuring that systems that need to connect to each other do so. In addition, to provide some measure of resource tracking and monitoring ability the library uses an SaaS monitoring service to keep track of system uptime and

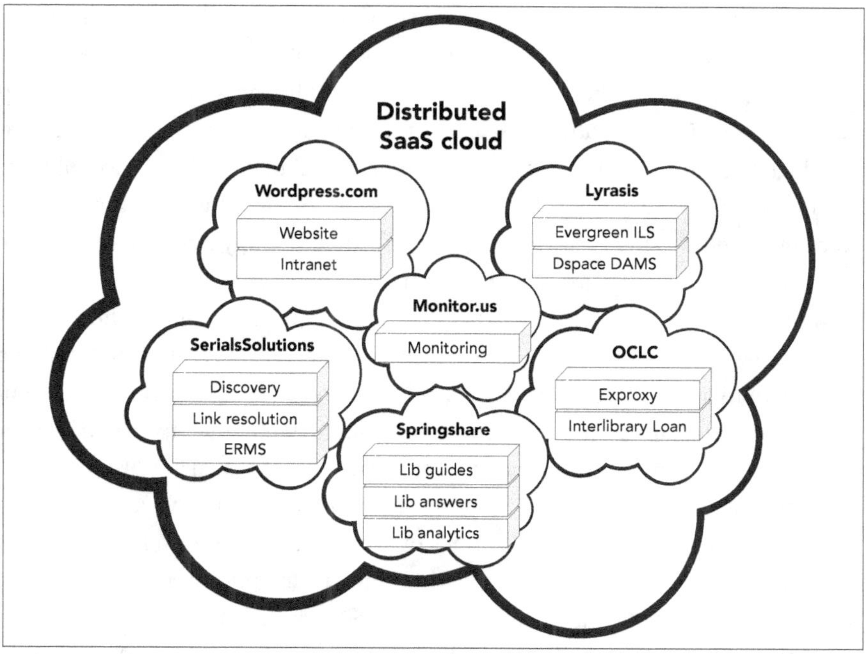

FIGURE 6.5
Distributed SaaS cloud services

deploys both its website and an internal intranet on a WordPress SaaS service. To provide authentication services, the library has negotiated relationships with its organizational IT to make LDAP authentication available to their hosted EZproxy service

Figure 6.5 does not attempt to show relationships between services and does not speculate on the database or application platforms of the services. The use of the staff intranet allows the library to track administrative accounts and URLs, store license and renewal data, and provide a database of subscribed services. In addition to working with organizational IT for LDAP authentication for specific services (e.g., EZproxy), the library must track IP addresses associated with each service, coordinate data services where needed (e.g., between Evergreen and serials management services), and work with organizational IT to manage DNS services so that a consistent site-naming scheme (e.g., catalog.library.edu, ezproxy.library.edu, www.library.edu) is employed across the wide range of service providers.

Some key advantages to this approach are efficiency and economies of scale for data-intensive services; enterprise-level IT support that does not depend on local expertise; SaaS monitoring and intranet services that facilitate auditing and management of providers; and achievement of rich information services without dependence on local IT resources. Although these solutions may be preferable for many libraries, the market is still somewhat limited in terms of product selection, and consolidating the number of vendors in this model comes at the expense of product selection. At the present time, libraries seeking to adopt SaaS solutions exclusively find themselves making decisions on both system functionality and vendor services. This is likely to change in the coming years as LIS providers optimize their software to run efficiently in the cloud.

For libraries seeking to use SaaS solutions to fill these gaps, there are an increasingly large number of case studies that explore SaaS alternatives to traditional library solutions. For example, Wilson (2011) explores the use of Drupal, Basecamp (http://basecamphq.com), and MIRA (http://atlassian.com/software/jira) as an alternative platform for electronic resource management systems. Wilson explores the challenges associated with adapting these platforms to serve a very specific function, as opposed to the implications of using an SaaS platform for this service, but the reported success of all three services point to an opportunity for these types of tools to have a dramatic impact on library IT decisions.

Perhaps the largest challenge in this adoption environment is managing the budgetary, license, identity management, and functional interoperability of these systems. Although many providers feature some form of integration through web-based plug-ins, back-end indexing, or automated data loading, making these services work together can be challenging, particularly for libraries interested in offloading as much technical work as possible. Unfortunately, these challenges may not emerge until a specific system is implemented or need found, and it can be difficult for libraries without in-house IT staff to identify potential solutions.

These data and interoperability problems do not have easy one-size-fits-all solutions, but there are potentially useful options. For example, Peter Murray (personal communication, March 2012) observed that Lyrasis tunes its hosting services based on library need and worked with outside consultants to bring data migration services to the table for libraries adopting its hosted IT services. In addition, there are IaaS providers whose primary purpose is to enable interoperability in an SaaS environment. Two examples are SnapLogic (http://snaplogic.com) and Jitterbit (http://jitterbit.com). These providers support data connections using a range of data sources (e.g., XML, CSV, ODBC), include a data migration design interface, and support HTTP endpoint services in which data queries and publishing actions can be activated by REST-based HTTP requests. These services require detailed data analysis skills; still, they may enable libraries to avoid costly IT infrastructure implementations for otherwise lightweight data transformation services.

■ ■ ■

These four approaches emphasize different strengths and weaknesses in cloud solutions and can serve as a starting point for libraries turning to the cloud. Approach one emphasizes the simplicity and control that comes with using a single cloud provider but recognizes the risk associated with being locked in through extensive use of provider APIs. Approach two seeks to mitigate some of this risk by using multiple providers and leveraging SaaS solutions to monitor, manage, and audit these providers. This approach illustrates the benefit of keeping track of cloud infrastructure and expenditures and suggests that SaaS solutions are a way to provide infrastructure management support. Approach three focuses on services that seek to abstract system design and implementation from IaaS providers and demonstrates the benefits of being able to use multiple cloud platforms easily; still, it is complex and likely to require IT and monetary resources beyond those of approaches one and two. Approach four recognizes that libraries may very likely turn to entirely SaaS-based solutions to address technology needs. In this case operational, administrative, and service quality issues are more important than technical issues.

In the real world, it is likely that libraries will employ more than one of these approaches. In fact, most libraries already rely to some extent on an SaaS provider or outsourced information service. In deciding whether to expand those roles or to consider other approaches when moving new services to the cloud, issues of local resources, expertise, IT support capacity, organizational policy, and service need are useful factors that can make one approach more viable than another. Regardless of the approach selected, IT service elements such as capacity planning, quality of service monitoring, service integration, and resource utilization monitoring are important elements of a sustainable IT infrastructure. The remainder of this chapter examines these issues and provides suggestions for getting started with cloud computing.

PREPARING FOR CLOUD COMPUTING ADOPTION

Library IT departments have grown in response to specific library needs such as client support, ILS support, and DAMS support. It is still common to find

IT librarians with backgrounds outside IT disciplines, but there is also a trend documented in library conferences and literature surrounding the adoption of industry-standard IT software development and service management approaches (Chang 2010; Dougherty 2009). These articles discuss the fact that libraries are adopting IT service models including formal models such as Information Technology Infrastructure Library (ITIL) (www.itil-officialsite.com) and less formal models such as ITSM (www.itsm.info/ITSM.htm). Even for libraries that have not used such models, there is use of service management portals (McHale 2010) and a growing awareness of the responsibility of community-driven software development (Reese 2012).

As our exploration of cloud approaches emphasizes, there is a need for formal IT management practices. For libraries turning mostly to SaaS solutions, the emphasis on IT management should be on maintaining an intranet of service providers and support information. For libraries turning more to PaaS and IaaS solutions, a more formal support strategy helps make the implementation and management of solutions sustainable. There are a variety of models from which to choose, including ITIL, the Systems Development Lifecycle (Department of Justice 2003), Control Objects for Information and Related Technology (ISACA 2011), and Microsoft Operations Framework (Microsoft 2011). These models help IT organizations approach system selection, development, implementation, management, and decommissioning of IT services in systematic ways and are helpful for libraries of any type. Although each model has its own distinct features, there have been attempts to find parallel processes and common ground (Pollard et al. 2009; Susanto et al. 2011) among them. Critics of these models point out that IT service model adoption has not demonstrated improvements in IT service and assert that they create administrative overhead and can lead to the creation of arbitrary boundaries (Addy 2007, 4).

Service management is a broad concept, defined as "a set of specialized organizational capabilities for providing value to customers in the form of services" (ITIL 2011, 11). The ITIL service life cycle describes the process of developing, delivering, and managing services and focuses in particular on knowledge management, SLAs, and standardization. Service management models can provide standardized measures of success including time to resolution, ratio of open and closed incidents, number of supported services, and time commitment of IT staff.

The ITIL service model, for example, discusses three stages of service: development, transition to production, and operational support. Each of these processes involves a wide range of discrete service components including defining service-level requirements, appraising IT support capacity, defining security requirements, and documenting user expectations. Addy (2007, 50) provides a full list of areas that require definition, including users, user requirements, expected deliverables, information or data provided by user, methods of service delivery, roles and responsibilities, contractual requirements, measures of success, definitions of service availability, measures of service capacity, security standards, and cost requirement/fulfillment. Although readers who are at the stage of incorporating formal IT service management approaches are best served by exploring each of these areas in more depth, it is important to be aware of these issues, if even informally, as your organization explores cloud solutions.

Each of the IT service models mentioned here work well in a cloud environment, but some are exploring issues specific to cloud adoption. The Microsoft Operations Framework (2011), for example, explores which system elements (e.g., networking, storage, data, applications) are locally or remotely managed in SaaS, PaaS, and IaaS environments. The best-practice recommendations for adopting common IT service guidelines to a cloud environment include changes to communication, servicing, and problem resolution. For example, the Microsoft guidelines suggest adding elemental cloud services to the service catalog to ensure that users understand what core cloud services are available and what their implementation costs and parameters are. Having documentation about the cloud platforms with which an organization has experience can help guide discussions and decisions surrounding IT service adoption and may prevent the use of multiple cloud service providers in a disjointed way. Microsoft's guidelines also suggest automating service and leveraging the self-service features of cloud platforms where possible.

For libraries engaged in a reappraisal of IT services, exploring a shift to cloud resources, or simply interested in finding ways to redesign their IT service approach, an understanding of IT service models and standards can help guide organizational change. This may lead to a centralized library IT, particularly in organizations that turn to PaaS or IaaS solutions, or it may lead to a more decentralized IT environment. In both cases the use of some form of service catalog, knowledge management system, and service ticket system can help libraries keep track of IT developments and make well-informed decisions about changes to their IT services. Despite the motivation to design the perfect system, system administrators should be tuned to the risk of overcommitting to complex system configurations and management practices. In fact, by using cloud environments to host service catalogs and knowledge management and ticket management systems, library IT departments can both capitalize on the efficiency benefits of SaaS solutions and demonstrate that they are willing to "eat their own dog food." The exercise of moving these internal services to the cloud or of deploying them in the cloud in the first place can also be a good testing ground for the implications of cloud service adoption in a library environment.

Although it is difficult to quantify the service capacity in an IT service department, the measures and frameworks that are part of IT service models can help measure the use of applications and resources. Likewise, when applied judiciously, these IT service models can expand the strengths of an IT department, enabling a small IT staff to manage an onslaught of requests more easily. Perhaps the most important principle of these service models is the view that IT service providers set boundaries and expectations that work for both customers and service providers. Although this is often formalized in SLAs, those agreements do not necessarily need to be complex and at the least can help avoid miscommunication and mismatches in customer expectations.

Make Room for New Services

For organizations exploring the cloud, one of the important questions is how cloud computing can help libraries support new or different services. There are several important IT and organizational issues to consider here, including service requirements, user expectations, IT platform options, cost considerations, and legal/organizational policies. Understanding where constraints and surpluses exist may help guide the discussion and help organizations understand where their energy is best allocated. For example, staffing constraints and lack of expertise may mean that libraries are tempted to turn to SaaS solutions. As the previous section points out, the use of SaaS solutions does not eliminate the need for IT service management tasks. In contrast, as libraries turn to more SaaS solutions, the need for a cross-departmental service catalog and knowledge/ticket management system increases. This need is even greater in organizations where the licensing, management, and deployment of SaaS services are distributed among multiple departments.

For organizations that find that the need for customized or localized services means the use of PaaS or IaaS, it can be useful to identify common or nondifferentiating services that are both high in resource utilization and low in impact and shift those services to SaaS solutions. This may include systems and services that were once the bread and butter of library IT departments, ILSs, and electronic resource management systems. Likewise, new library services such as large-scale discovery, resource recommendation, and resource sharing depend on network-based services to such an extent that they work only as an SaaS solution.

Build Support for the Migration

Some of the major internal limitations of moving to cloud computing include local policy, staff expertise, lack of cooperation with organizational IT, lack of funding, and lack of satisfaction with provider terms. Many of these issues require administrative-level work with providers; nevertheless, understanding and addressing the limitations of current staff expertise through new recruitment or training can dramatically improve an organization's ability to adopt cloud solutions. It is not necessarily easy, but building internal capacity for software programming, IT service, and server administration increases the number of options in IT adoption and facilitates management of SaaS as well as PaaS and IaaS solutions.

Organizational resistance to cloud migration can be difficult to overcome. Marketing the shift as an opportunity to redefine service relations between libraries and organizational IT or to enable new collaborations can help resistant departments see how cloud adoption can benefit them. Libraries moving to the cloud are likely to depend on some key services from their organization's IT, including DNS resolution, firewall support (for both incoming and outgoing ports as needed), and advice on IT issues. It makes sense for libraries to be well informed about legal and policy issues before heading to IT departments and to be prepared to take on the liability of service uptime and capacity planning in a formal document. Often, IT organizations are guided by a need to define and understand service boundaries. By recognizing these boundaries and taking appropriate responsibility, libraries can often be successful in renegotiating a relationship with organizational IT management that is beneficial for both parties.

Leverage Vendor-Provided Tools

One of the key advantages of adopting cloud services is the built-in service infrastructure that comes with even the most basic services. For example, Amazon has a site dedicated to informing cloud customers about value-added applications (http://aws.amazon.com/customerapps/). These services include mobile AWS management tools such as iAWSManager and value-added services such as

LabSlice—a virtual computing lab (VCL) management tool designed to facilitate the design and deployment of VCL infrastructure on AWS. Many of the SaaS, PaaS, and IaaS platforms discussed in this book feature robust web-based management interfaces that are designed with mobile device utilization in mind. For those services that do not work well in a web-based mobile interface, there are often mobile device applications that provide access. For example, Linode services include an iPhone management application called Linode Manager, and Android apps that were not developed by Linode but leverage the Linode API suite are available.

Choosing applications to tie into or provide advanced services on top of cloud providers can be difficult. Mobile management tools, alternative client-based access tools such as Cyberduck, and application monitoring and auditing tools are of high value and pose little risk to the core cloud services. As in the case of cloud-based digital object storage, however, it can be difficult to use some cloud functions without relying heavily on third-party products. Perhaps the most important consideration is not whether a service adds value, since most of them do, but rather whether there is a second pathway away from the service if there is some failure of the primary application. For example, though using Amazon S3 as a file system through Cyberduck or S3-Fuse (http://sourceforge.net/projects/s3fuse/) serves a valuable need, adopters need some method by which they can recover their data if the selected service fails. In this case, there are several tools, not the least of which is Amazon's own API toolkit, which can help with object recovery.

Stand on the Shoulders of Giants

One of the great advantages of moving to the cloud is gaining access to enterprise-level IT services with very little overhead. Another important advantage is the ability to tap into support communities in both the cloud and library IT world. Many of the cloud providers discussed in this book make their tutorials available freely and even provide free levels of service for new adopters. In addition, there are companies such as Alestic (http://alestic.com) and willing experts in the library community (e.g., Code4Lib, LITA, and ALA Cloud Computing interest group) that can help answer questions, give advice, or solve specific technical problems. There is also an abundance of white papers, guides, tutorials, best-practice recommendations, and getting-started documents available to new and experienced cloud users.

A challenge that staff new to server administration in general are likely to encounter is developing an understanding of how to work with the many moving parts of system security, performance, application management, and IT service. Linode's system documentation and Mitchell's AWS-focused 2011 LITA preconference tutorials (http://erikmitchell.info/lita_2011_aws/aws_tutorials.pdf) can serve as initial guides through these environments. Many companies also publish a series of higher-level guides, video tutorials, and webinars intended to help adopters implement secure services. For example, Amazon's white paper series (http://aws.amazon.com/whitepapers) includes operational checklists, case studies on backup and recovery, and overviews of security and compliance procedures. Linode also offers a wide range of useful tutorials (http://library.linode.com). Linode's documentation library naturally focuses on managing Linode's infrastructure, but it includes platform-agnostic tutorials on how to create high-availability applications, set up system security, and deploy application frameworks. Because Linode's documentation often includes tailored tutorials for Ubuntu, Fedora, CentOS, and other flavors of Linux, it helps readers understand both the broad concepts of system administration and the specific practices associated with a given platform. For users seeking to take advantage of PaaS solutions, both Heroku (http://devcenter.heroku.com/) and Amazon (http://aws.amazon.com/articles) include platform-specific tutorials on deploying applications in their environment.

Get Started

This book outlines several approaches to cloud computing or virtualization, focusing on technical, organizational, and environmental factors that influence decision making in this area. For those libraries seeking to implement new services, cloud computing can provide a way to implement those services quickly and without considerable overhead for organizational IT. In contrast, libraries that are looking toward cloud computing as a way to transform existing IT practice are best served by examining their current IT service environment as well as the functional needs of their user community and then selecting cloud solutions that will both improve service quality and create room for new information services.

Library-specific systems are moving toward the cloud, and there are new opportunities for libraries to engage with industry-standard applications. The trend toward cloud computing has become mainstream in both the library and wider information community, and, although library adoption of cloud computing lags behind the corporate world, a robust range of services is available. Libraries are more frequently turning to SaaS than to PaaS or IaaS solutions. It should not be surprising that libraries are finding SaaS solutions attractive, given the benefits of economies of scale, potential cost savings, and improved service offerings. Issues of expertise, local capacity, organizational policy, and desired end-user service outcomes are also heavily influencing these choices. This trend toward SaaS poses both opportunities for libraries and challenges to open-data and open-source communities in the library world. In fact, as libraries turn increasingly to cloud solutions, they are helping redefine our industry's view of distinctive library services and shaping the design of new information systems. If nothing else, the shift to SaaS platforms is demonstrating that just about every library service can be turned into a generalized commodity whose primary purpose is to support high-quality user-facing services. Still, issues of data ownership, resource sharing, and interoperability pose continued challenges for these communities as library IT vendors seek to offer more comprehensive service frameworks that discourage multivendor adoption.

In contrast, PaaS and IaaS solutions provide a great level of flexibility, independence, and assurance of privacy at lower cost but at the expense of more local investment and expertise. There are few ready-to-use library-specific applications in these environments. This points to a real opportunity for open-source communities, consortia, and commercial providers to expand their support for PaaS and IaaS solutions and to help libraries make use of a wider range of cloud services.

REFERENCES

Addy, Rob. 2007. *Effective IT Service Management: To ITIL and Beyond!* New York: Springer.

Amazon. 2012. "Deploying Applications: AWS CloudFormation." *Amazon Web Service Documentation.* http://docs.amazonwebservices.com/AWSCloudFormation/latest/UserGuide/deploying.applications.html.

Chan, Jason. 2012. "Cloud Security @ Netflix." *SVForum Cloud and Virtualization SIG,* March 27, 2012. www.slideshare.net/jason_chan/cloud-security-at-netflix.

Chang, May. 2010. "An Agile Approach to Library IT Innovations." *Library Hi Tech* 28 (no. 4): 672–89. doi:10.1108/07378831011096303.

Cockroft, Adrian. 2012. "Cloud Architecture at Netflix: How Netflix Built a Scalable Java Oriented PaaS Running on AWS." *SVForum,* March 27, 2012. www.slideshare.net/adrianco/netflix-in-the-cloud-at-sv-forum.

Cockroft, Adrian, Cory Hicks, and Greg Orzell. 2011. "Lessons Netflix Learned from the AWS Outage." *Netflix Tech Blog,* April 2011. http://techblog.netflix.com/2011_04_01_archive.html.

Department of Justice. 2003. Department of Justice Systems Development Life Cycle Guidance Document. January. www.justice.gov/jmd/irm/lifecycle/table.htm.

Dougherty, William. C. 2009. "Virtualization and Libraries: The Future Is Now (or Virtualization: Whither Libraries or Libraries Wither?)." *Journal of Academic Librarianship* 35 (no. 3): 274–76. doi:10.1016/j.acalib.2009.03.006.

Feid, Allen. 2012. "Using Amazon's CloudFormation, Cloud-Init, Chef and Fog to Automate Infrastructure." *Allan Feid blog*, March 2, 2012. http://allanfeid.com/content/using-amazons-cloudformation-cloud-init-chef-and-fog-automate-infrastructure.

ISACA. 2011. "COBIT Framework for IT Governance and Control." ISACA website. www.isaca.org/Knowledge-Center/cobit/Pages.

ITIL. 2011. *ITIL: Service Design*. Norwich, Norfolk, U.K.: The Stationary Office.

McHale, Nina. 2010. "Managing Library IT Workflow with Bugzilla." *Code4Lib Journal* 11. http://journal.code4lib.org/articles/3814.

Microsoft. 2011. Microsoft Operations Framework 4.0. 2011. Microsoft Operations Framework, last modified October 27, 2011. http://technet.microsoft.com/en-us/library/cc506049.aspx.

Pollard, Carol. E., Dhiraj Gupta, and John W. Satzinger. 2009. "Integrating SDLC and ITSM to 'Servitize' Systems Development." *AMCIS 2009 Proceedings*. http://aisel.aisnet.org/amcis2009/415.

Reese, Terry. 2012. "Purposeful Development: Being Ready When Your Project Moves from 'Hobby' to Mission Critical." *Code4Lib Journal* 16. http://journal.code4lib.org/articles/6393.

Susanto, Heru, Mohammad Nabil Almunawar, and Yong Chee Tuan. 2011. "Information Security Management System Standards: A Comparative Study of the Big Five." *International Journal of Electrical and Computer Sciences* 5:23–29. www.ijens.org/Vol_11_I_05/113505-6969-IJECS-IJENS.pdf.

Tonjes, Chris. 2011. "Amazon Fail: DC Public Library's Lessons Learned from the Amazon Cloud Outage." American Library Association Annual Conference, July 2011. http://connect.ala.org/files/dcpl%20cloud%20computing%20amazon%20fail.pdf.

Wilson, Kristen. 2011. "Beyond Library Software: New Tools for Electronic Resources Management." *Serials Review* 37 (no. 4): 294–304. doi:10.1016/j.serrev.2011.09.010.

INDEX

S